Matt's
KITCHEN
GARDEN
Cookbook

MATT MORAN

Photography by Rob Palmer

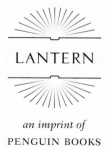

LANTERN

an imprint of
PENGUIN BOOKS

To all the amazing producers
who go above and beyond to provide
the best and freshest ingredients.
Without your passion and commitment,
chefs and restaurateurs like myself
wouldn't be where we are today.

Introduction

What I really love about being a chef is that I'm always learning; exploring new ideas and trying different things. I've now been in the profession for over twenty-five years and, while I've long had an appreciation for locally grown produce, it has recently become more of a focus for me. Owning a farm and producing my own lamb and beef for the restaurants has been an important part of my cooking for many years, but creating the kitchen garden at my restaurant Chiswick really opened my eyes and made me more aware of seasonality – what we should be eating and when.

Of course, this increasing interest in growing our own food is not limited to those in the restaurant industry. In recent years there has been a huge rise in the number of community gardens, which bring people together from all walks of life and ethnic backgrounds to plant, tend and harvest their own produce. And having put in the hard yards to grow the food themselves, people are again learning to value what they are eating.

This also applies to all the children who are benefiting from school kitchen gardens. These kids are learning where food actually comes from and are taking responsibility for producing it. With this comes an unbeatable sense of pride in knowing that they grew and, in many cases, cooked the food themselves. We owe a great deal to Stephanie Alexander for initiating her Kitchen Garden Program and encouraging kids to get their hands dirty and work together to achieve a common goal.

More and more restaurants have their own gardens now, too. The heart of Chiswick is its garden, and our menu changes according to what is flourishing in it. We enjoy the challenge of tailoring the menu to highlight our seasonal produce – letting it shine when it's at its very best.

I've had a kitchen garden at home for several years now. There's nothing more fulfilling than growing something yourself and then cooking with it – it just tastes better. The push for growing food locally is something I truly believe in, and there's no reason why everybody can't be doing it. Even if you live in an apartment, growing herbs in a pot on the windowsill can make a difference. I promise you that pesto made using freshly picked basil (see my recipe on page 80) will always taste better.

My passion for cooking has not lessened over the years – quite the opposite, in fact. The incredible diversity of produce available to us now inspires me every day, and our connection to that produce is really starting to evolve. Of course, we can't be expected to grow everything ourselves, but what we should be doing is sourcing ingredients responsibly, from local growers and farmers' markets. It's a privilege to meet the people producing our food, to hear what they have to say about their produce and to learn from them. One of the main reasons I wanted to make the television series *Paddock to Plate* was to showcase these amazing, passionate producers and share their stories.

The recipes in this book all celebrate fresh, locally grown produce, and I've tried to keep them fairly simple to allow the key seasonal ingredients to take centre stage. Many of the dishes are designed to share with family and friends – I love this casual and relaxed form of entertaining. I generally start with some nibbles and small plates, then move onto shared plates and sides or salads. The slow-cooked lamb with hummus, tomato salad and mint salsa (see page 102) is always well received, as is my seafood tagine with saffron couscous (see page 107).

Sometimes an occasion calls for a little more structure, with a specific starter and main meal. I enjoy this style of entertaining just as much, and have some great suggestions in the small plates and mains chapters. No meal is complete without something sweet to finish, whether it be a light and pretty concoction of berries and meringue with passionfruit curd (see page 166) or a richly satisfying Caramélia éclair (see page 164), and there are lots of options in the sweet chapter.

As anybody with a garden will know, an abundance of a particular fruit or vegetable can sometimes be a little overwhelming – there's only so much you can give away to friends and neighbours! This is where preserving comes into its own (see page 191). It gives you the chance to capture your homegrown produce at its seasonal best and enjoy it all year round.

However you choose to cook, I think the key is to respect nature's bounty and enjoy the luxury of really fresh ingredients. I hope you enjoy the recipes that follow as much as I enjoyed writing them.

MATT

1

Nibbles

Spicy bite-sized morsels; crunchy, piquant pickled vegetables; and plenty of sliders and sambos for when you want something more substantial – all perfect for passing around on a platter and enjoying with drinks.

½ cauliflower

12 baby (Dutch) carrots, trimmed and peeled

pickling liquid (see page 208), to cover

4 red radishes, trimmed and quartered

1 stalk celery, trimmed, peeled and cut on the diagonal into batons

1 teaspoon extra virgin olive oil, plus extra to serve

pinch of sugar

pinch of salt

edible flowers, to garnish

Dukkah

300 ml vegetable oil

50 g wild rice

1 teaspoon coriander seeds

1 teaspoon fennel seeds

1 teaspoon cumin seeds

1 teaspoon white peppercorns

½ cup (80 g) sunflower seeds

½ cup (80 g) pumpkin seeds (pepitas)

½ cup (75 g) pistachios

1 teaspoon salt flakes

Avocado puree

½ avocado, stone removed

½ lemon, juiced

1 teaspoon olive oil

pinch of wasabi powder

salt and pepper

Pickled vegetables with dukkah

This is a stunning dish, both in appearance and flavour. Use a variety of carrots if you can, such as yellow, orange and purple – we've been growing them in the garden at Chiswick and the colours and flavours are fantastic. Purple cauliflower also works really well here, if you can get your hands on some – half the amount in purple and the rest in green or white would look great. For the radishes, I'd suggest using French breakfast or cherry belle. If you have any dukkah left over, serve it with bread and olive oil or sprinkle it over roasted vegetables or labne.

Serves 4

1   Break up the cauliflower into small florets. Place the cauliflower and carrots in two separate heatproof bowls (if you have purple carrots and/or cauliflower they need to go in separate bowls as the colour may bleed a little). Pour enough hot pickling liquid over the cauliflower and carrots to cover. Cover the bowls with plastic film and set aside until the vegetables and liquid have cooled.

2   Meanwhile, to make the dukkah, preheat the oven to 180°C.

3   Line a tray with paper towel and set a fine-meshed sieve over a stainless-steel bowl. Heat the vegetable oil in a large, heavy-based frying pan over high heat until it starts smoking. Carefully add the rice – it will puff up. Give it a quick stir, then transfer to the sieve. Spread the puffed rice over the lined tray to drain. Discard the oil once cooled.

4   Toast the coriander seeds, fennel seeds, cumin seeds and white peppercorns in a clean, dry frying pan over medium heat until aromatic. Transfer the spices to a mortar and pound with the pestle to a coarse powder. Place in a bowl.

5   Place the seeds and pistachios on a baking tray and roast for 5–8 minutes or until the nuts are aromatic. Remove from the oven. Roughly chop the seeds and nuts (this could also be done by briefly pulsing in a food processor). Add to the spices with the puffed rice and salt flakes and mix well. Set aside.

6   To make the avocado puree, scoop out the flesh of the avocado and place in a blender with the lemon juice, olive oil, wasabi powder and 2½ tablespoons water. Blend until smooth, then season with salt and pepper, to taste. Press the puree through a fine-meshed sieve into a bowl.

7   Place the radish and celery in a bowl and add the olive oil, sugar and salt. Toss to combine. Drain the cauliflower and carrots. Cut the carrots in half lengthways (or into quarters if large). Arrange all the vegetables on a serving plate and drop spoonfuls of avocado puree in and around them. Using a spoon, place a line of the dukkah in front of the vegetables. Drizzle the vegetables with the extra olive oil, sprinkle with salt and garnish with the edible flowers, then serve.

12 small bread rolls

3 vine-ripened tomatoes, thickly sliced

½ head red oakleaf lettuce, leaves separated and torn

½ head green oakleaf lettuce, leaves separated and torn

12 white anchovies

Veal patties

640 g veal chuck steak, coarsely minced

80 g pork fat, coarsely minced

½ bunch flat-leaf parsley, chopped

1 teaspoon salt

1 teaspoon onion powder

1 teaspoon ground white pepper

1 cup (150 g) plain flour

150 g panko breadcrumbs

2 eggs

2½ tablespoons milk

200 ml vegetable oil

Sauce gribiche

160 g mayonnaise (see page 211)

3 tablespoons diced cornichons

3 tablespoons pickled capers

1 golden shallot, roughly chopped

finely grated zest of ½ lemon

½ bunch flat-leaf parsley, finely chopped

Veal sliders

These little beauties are incredibly more-ish. Sauce gribiche is a take on tartare sauce, and it's also delicious with fish and chips. We have used milk buns, the type you buy from Asian bakeries, but you could use any small rolls – mini brioche buns would be lovely.

Makes 12

1 To make the sauce gribiche, place all the ingredients in a bowl and stir until combined. Cover and place in the fridge until required.

2 To make the veal patties, use your hands to combine the minced veal and pork fat in a bowl. Add the parsley, salt, onion powder and pepper and mix until well combined. Divide the mixture into 12 portions and shape each into a patty.

3 Place the flour and breadcrumbs in two separate bowls. Crack the eggs into a third bowl, add the milk and lightly whisk together. Lightly coat each patty in flour, then egg mixture, allowing the excess to drip off. Place in the breadcrumbs and turn to coat.

4 Heat the vegetable oil in a large heavy-based frying pan over medium–high heat. Cook the patties, in batches if necessary to avoid crowding the pan, until golden brown, about 2–3 minutes. Flip the patties and cook the other side until golden brown. Transfer to paper towel to drain.

5 Cut the bread rolls in half and toast the cut sides of each. Spread a dollop of the sauce gribiche over each base. Divide the tomato, lettuce, anchovies and veal patties among the bases. Cover with the tops of the rolls and serve.

10 roman beans, trimmed and quartered

pickling liquid (see page 208), to cover

½ cup (80 g) black kalamata olives, pitted

80 g green kalamata olives, pitted

flatbread (such as rosemary flatbread, page 23), to serve

salt flakes, to serve

Tomato and mustard sauce

3 cm knob ginger, peeled

1 clove garlic

½ long red chilli

2 teaspoons olive oil

½ teaspoon black mustard seeds

pinch of ground turmeric

pinch of saffron threads

2 teaspoons white wine vinegar

1 tablespoon grated palm sugar

1 tablespoon fish sauce

2½ tablespoons chicken stock (see page 206)

200 g tomato sauce (see page 209)

Olives and pickled beans with tomato and mustard sauce

The tomato and mustard sauce here is really spicy and aromatic, just the thing to lift the pickled beans. You could easily serve this up as a side dish, too, for a piece of fish or barbecued meat.

Serves 4

1 Place the beans in a saucepan and add enough pickling liquid to cover. Bring to the boil over high heat, then remove and set aside, covered, until the beans and liquid have cooled.

2 To make the tomato and mustard sauce, put the ginger, garlic and chilli into a mortar and pound with the pestle to a coarse paste. Heat the olive oil in a heavy-based saucepan over medium–high heat. Add the mustard seeds and cook for 1–2 minutes or until they start popping. Add the ginger paste and cook for 2 minutes, then add the turmeric and saffron and cook for 2 minutes more, stirring to prevent the paste sticking to the base of the pan. Add the vinegar, palm sugar and fish sauce and cook for 2 minutes, until reduced. Add the stock and tomato sauce and bring to the boil, then reduce the heat to low and simmer, stirring occasionally, for 10 minutes or until thickened slightly.

3 Drain the beans from the pickling liquid and add to the tomato sauce with the olives. Bring to a simmer, then transfer to a bowl and serve hot with flatbread, sprinkled with salt flakes.

12 sweet pickled gherkins

12 small bread rolls

½ cup (150 g) Japanese mayonnaise

½ head green coral lettuce, leaves separated and torn

Alaskan crab patties

480 g cooked Alaskan king crabmeat

3 golden shallots, thinly sliced

½ bunch coriander, leaves finely chopped

3 tablespoons Japanese mayonnaise

juice of 1½ lemons

salt and pepper

1 cup (150 g) plain flour

150 g panko breadcrumbs

2 eggs

2½ tablespoons milk

100 ml vegetable oil

Alaskan crab sliders

This dish has been on the Chiswick menu since we opened and it's very popular – we took it off at one point and had complaints from guests, so it's there for good now. Alaskan crabmeat has an amazing texture and flavour – it's well worth tracking down from a quality seafood supplier.

Makes 12

1 Thinly slice the gherkins, then cut into thin strips. Set aside.

2 To make the Alaskan crab patties, put the crabmeat into a bowl and use your hands to shred, removing any fragments of shell. Add the shallot, coriander, mayonnaise and lemon juice and mix until combined. Taste and season with salt and pepper. Divide the mixture into 12 portions and shape each into a patty.

3 Place the flour and breadcrumbs in two separate bowls. Crack the eggs into a third bowl, add the milk and lightly whisk together. Lightly coat each patty in flour, then egg mixture, allowing the excess to drip off. Place in the breadcrumbs and turn to coat.

4 Heat the vegetable oil in a heavy-based frying pan over medium–high heat. Cook the patties, in batches if necessary to avoid crowding the pan, until golden brown, about 1–2 minutes. Flip the patties and cook the other side until golden brown. Transfer to paper towel to drain and sprinkle with salt.

5 Cut the bread rolls in half and toast the cut sides of each. Spread a dollop of the mayonnaise over each top and base. Divide the lettuce, gherkin and crab patties among the bases. Cover with the tops of the rolls and serve.

12 oysters, freshly shucked

½ bunch chives, finely chopped

rock salt, to serve

Lemon and ginger dressing

2½ tablespoons chardonnay wine

2½ tablespoons chardonnay vinegar

2½ tablespoons rice wine vinegar

2 tablespoons sugar syrup (see page 211)

1 lemon, zest removed in wide strips

1 cm knob ginger, peeled and finely grated

Candied lemon zest

1 lemon, zest removed in wide strips

100 ml sugar syrup (see page 211)

Oysters with lemon and ginger dressing

I love a freshly shucked oyster, and the combination of flavours in this dressing – citrus and a hint of ginger – complements them perfectly. My grandfather was an oyster farmer and he always told me that you don't like your first oyster, you like your tenth. I encourage all our kitchen staff to try oysters a few times at least.

Serves 4

1 To make the lemon and ginger dressing, bring the wine to the boil in a small heavy-based saucepan over high heat. Flambe the wine – that is, set it alight to burn off the alcohol. When the flame goes out, add the vinegars and sugar syrup and return to the boil. Add the lemon zest and ginger, then remove from the heat and leave to infuse for 10 minutes. Strain the liquid through a fine-meshed sieve into a bowl and set aside.

2 For the candied lemon zest, remove all the pith from the lemon zest and cut the zest into small thin strips. Place in a small heavy-based saucepan with the sugar syrup over low heat. Slowly bring to a gentle simmer, then hold at a simmer for 15–20 minutes, until tender. Remove from the heat and let the zest cool in the syrup. Once cooled, use a slotted spoon to remove the zest from the syrup.

3 Spoon a teaspoon of the dressing over each oyster and top with some candied lemon zest and chives. Serve on a bed of rock salt.

750 g skinless boneless pork shoulder

2 litres master stock (see page 207)

12 small bread rolls

Coleslaw

1 green apple, peeled and cored

½ red onion, thinly sliced

¼ green cabbage, cored and finely shredded

3 spring onions, trimmed and thinly sliced

100 ml classic dressing (see page 210)

3 tablespoons mayonnaise (see page 211)

salt and pepper

Pulled pork sliders

This pulled pork is so simple to make and the flavour is just sensational, with the apple coleslaw adding a lovely sweetness. You can cook it the day before if you like – leave it in the stock and keep it in the fridge, then return to the boil to warm it up before using.

Makes 12

1 Preheat the oven to 150°C.

2 Place the pork in an ovenproof saucepan, cover with the master stock (top up with water if necessary to ensure the pork is submerged) and bring to a simmer over medium heat. Skim off any impurities, then cover with a cartouche (a round of baking paper) and put into the oven for 2 hours or until the meat flakes when tested with a fork. Remove from the oven and leave the pork in the liquid until it is cool enough to handle.

3 Meanwhile, to make the coleslaw, cut the apple into matchsticks and place in a mixing bowl with the onion, cabbage, spring onion, classic dressing and mayonnaise. Toss until combined, then taste and season with salt and pepper.

4 Take the pork out of the pan and shred. Put the pork into a heavy-based frying pan with 100 ml of the stock it was cooked in and cook over medium heat for 2–3 minutes, until warmed through.

5 Cut the bread rolls in half and toast the cut sides of each. Put some coleslaw on the bases, then the shredded pork and top with the remaining coleslaw. Cover with the tops of the rolls and serve.

2 long red chillies, thinly sliced

400 g squid hoods, cleaned

vegetable oil, for deep-frying

⅓ cup (50 g) plain flour

micro-coriander or young coriander leaves, to garnish

lime cheeks, to serve

Salt mix

2 tablespoons table salt

1 tablespoon ground white pepper

1 tablespoon ground Sichuan pepper

Chilli salt squid

The trick here is to make the cooking hot and quick, which gives the squid a lovely crisp coating and melt-in-your-mouth texture. The fresher the squid, the better the result will be. I live by a little bay in Sydney and sometimes I take my son Harry, who's twelve, down there to go squidding, especially around Christmas time. There's nothing quite like squid that is caught and cooked that same day.

Serves 4

1   Preheat the oven to 140°C. Put the chilli on a baking tray lined with baking paper and bake for 10–15 minutes, until dried. Set aside.

2   Use a sharp knife to separate the wings from the squid hoods, then cut each hood in half lengthways. Lightly score the inside of each hood in a diamond pattern, then cut into triangular pieces.

3   To make the salt mix, place all the ingredients in a bowl and mix well.

4   Preheat a deep-fryer to 180°C, or half-fill a large heavy-based saucepan with vegetable oil and heat over medium–high heat to 180°C (a cube of bread will brown in 20 seconds). Toss the squid in the flour to coat, then gently lower into the hot oil and fry for 3–4 minutes, until golden. Transfer to paper towel to drain and sprinkle with the salt mix. Serve scattered with the dried chilli and coriander, and with lime cheeks alongside.

10 g salted butter, softened

8 thick slices rye bread

4 sweet dill pickles, thinly sliced

80 g sliced gruyere

Corned beef

500 g silverside, trimmed

ice cubes

½ onion, roughly chopped

½ stalk celery, roughly chopped

½ leek, green part only, washed and roughly chopped

½ carrot, roughly chopped

3 cloves garlic

2 bay leaves

4 sprigs thyme

4 cloves

Sauerkraut

2 cups (500 ml) white vinegar

⅓ cup (100 g) rock salt

45 g caster sugar

2 long red chillies, roughly chopped

1 clove garlic, crushed

1 bay leaf

½ teaspoon coriander seeds, crushed

pinch of ground white pepper

1 clove

½ green cabbage, cored and shredded

Thousand island dressing

200 g mayonnaise (see page 211)

80 g finely chopped sweet dill pickles

2 small golden shallots, finely chopped

juice of ½ lemon

1 tablespoon tomato sauce (ketchup)

1 teaspoon Worcestershire sauce

pinch of sweet paprika

grated fresh horseradish, to taste

Tabasco sauce, to taste

Reuben sandwiches

This sandwich is a New York classic and it's a must-try for anyone heading over there – you'll find a superb version at Katz's Delicatessen, where they shot the infamous scene in *When Harry Met Sally*. Thousand island dressing might seem like an odd addition, but believe me, it works. Once made, the corned beef, sauerkraut and dressing can all be kept in airtight containers in the fridge. Then, you can knock up a Reuben whenever you choose (daily, if you're anything like me!). If you can get your hands on some David Blackmore wagyu silverside for this, I'd highly recommend it.

Serves 4

1   To make the corned beef, put the silverside into an airtight container and cover with iced water. Cover and place in the fridge for 3 hours, then drain and rinse well. Place in a large heavy-based saucepan and cover with cold water. Slowly bring to a simmer over low heat, then skim off any impurities. Add the rest of the ingredients and simmer for 2–3 hours or until tender. Leave the silverside to cool completely in the liquid.

2   For the sauerkraut, put 2.5 litres water into a large heavy-based saucepan and add the vinegar, salt, sugar, chilli, garlic, bay leaf, coriander seeds, pepper and clove. Bring to the boil over medium heat, then strain through a fine-meshed sieve set over a bowl. Discard the solids. Return the liquid to the pan and return to the boil over medium heat. Add the cabbage and simmer for 12 minutes, then remove from the heat and cool the cabbage completely in the liquid.

3   To make the thousand island dressing, combine the mayonnaise, pickle, shallot, lemon juice, tomato sauce, Worcestershire and paprika in a bowl. Stir in the horseradish and Tabasco, to taste.

4   Heat a sandwich press. Drain the corned beef and thinly slice. Butter half the slices of bread and top with a generous amount of drained sauerkraut, then some sliced dill pickle, corned beef and gruyere. Butter the remaining slices of bread and place on top. Place in the hot sandwich press until the cheese has melted, then remove and gently open each sandwich. Add 2 tablespoons of the dressing to each and some more dill pickle, then close and serve.

Pan-roasted padrón peppers

2½ tablespoons vegetable oil

12 padrón peppers

2½ tablespoons sherry vinegar

salt flakes, to serve

lemon cheeks, to serve

Pan-roasted padrón peppers

These small green Spanish peppers are now being grown in Australia and are great to barbecue and finish with lemon juice and salt. It's said that one in ten can be extremely hot, but I think those are pretty good odds!

Serves 4

1   Heat the oil in a large frying pan over high heat until it just starts to smoke. Add the peppers (be careful as the hot oil will spit) and cook, turning often, until blistered all over and blackened in places. Transfer to a serving dish and pour over the vinegar, then sprinkle with salt flakes and serve hot, with lemon cheeks.

---

1 bulb confit garlic (see page 194)

2 sprigs rosemary, leaves picked

extra virgin olive oil, for brushing

salt flakes, to serve

Pizza dough

1⅔ cups (250 g) plain flour, plus extra for dusting

5 g dry yeast

1 teaspoon salt

Rosemary flatbread

Flatbread are so versatile and make a great accompaniment for all sorts of dishes. If you'd like to cook these in one go, place the dough on two large baking trays sprayed with oil and swap the trays around halfway through cooking. You can use other herbs, such as tarragon or oregano, instead of rosemary.

Makes 4

1   To make the pizza dough, put the flour, yeast, salt and ⅔ cup (160 ml) lukewarm water in an electric mixer with a dough hook and mix until the dough is just starting to come together. Turn out onto a floured benchtop and lightly knead just until it is smooth and elastic (take care not to overwork it). Place the dough in a lightly floured bowl and cover with plastic film. Leave in a warm, draught-free place for 2 hours to prove, until doubled in size, then gently knock it back.

2   Place a pizza stone in the oven and preheat to 240°C (or 280°C if you have a wood-fired oven).

3   Divide the pizza dough into four portions. Carefully roll or stretch one portion into a round, roughly 15 cm in diameter. Drain the confit garlic in a fine-meshed sieve. Use a spoon to mash the garlic, then spread a quarter of it in a thin layer over the dough. Sprinkle over a quarter of the rosemary leaves.

4   Put the flatbread on the hot pizza stone and bake for 5–6 minutes or until golden brown and crispy. Finish the bread by brushing with a little extra virgin olive oil and sprinkling with salt flakes. Cut into wedges and serve. Repeat to cook the remaining flatbread.

^ Rosemary flatbread

2 duck eggs

ice cubes

⅔ cup (100 g) plain flour

2 cups (100 g) panko breadcrumbs

2 chicken eggs

2½ tablespoons milk

vegetable oil, for deep-frying

1 bunch salad onions, stems trimmed
and quartered

2½ tablespoons olive oil

salt and pepper

micro-coriander or young coriander
leaves, to garnish

3 tablespoons Japanese mayonnaise

Pickled mushrooms

50 g enoki mushrooms, trimmed

50 g shiitake mushrooms, trimmed
and quartered

75 g shimeji mushrooms, trimmed

pickling liquid (see page 208), to cover

Scotch egg mince

2 tablespoons olive oil

¼ long red chilli, seeded and finely chopped

½ clove garlic, finely chopped

1 teaspoon finely chopped ginger

200 g duck sausages, skin removed

½ cooked peking duck breast,
finely chopped

¼ onion, finely diced

1 small chicken egg, lightly beaten

1 tablespoon oyster sauce

1 teaspoon sesame oil

1 sprig coriander, chopped

1 tablespoon panko breadcrumbs

pinch of ground white pepper

pinch of dried chilli flakes

salt and pepper

Peking duck scotch eggs

I love the idea of scotch eggs, as they're such an interesting way to use mince. You can find duck eggs at any good butcher – they're beautifully rich. It can be somewhat of a challenge to get them perfectly cooked inside the coating, so don't be disappointed if you don't nail it the first time. With a little practice you'll get the feel for it. If you have some ginger and shallot sauce (see page 210) handy, you could use it in the mince instead of the oyster sauce.

Serves 4

1   To make the pickled mushrooms, put all the mushrooms into a heatproof bowl and pour over enough hot pickling liquid to cover. Cover the bowl with plastic film and set aside until the mushrooms and liquid have cooled.

2   Meanwhile, bring a saucepan of water to a rapid boil over high heat. Gently add the duck eggs and cook for 7 minutes, then transfer to a bowl of iced water to stop the cooking process. When the eggs have cooled, carefully peel away the shells. Set aside.

3   Preheat the oven to 180°C.

4   To make the scotch egg mince, heat the olive oil in a frying pan over medium heat and saute the chilli, garlic and ginger for 2–3 minutes, until softened. Place in a mixing bowl. Add the remaining ingredients and mix until well combined. Divide into 2 portions and shape each into a flat patty. Place a boiled duck egg on the centre of each and wrap the mince around to fully enclose.

5   Place the flour and breadcrumbs in two separate bowls. Crack the chicken eggs into a third bowl, add the milk and lightly whisk together. Lightly coat each scotch egg in flour, then egg mixture, allowing the excess to drip off. Place in the breadcrumbs and turn to coat. Repeat to make a double coating.

6   Preheat a deep-fryer to 180°C, or half-fill a large heavy-based saucepan with vegetable oil and heat over medium–high heat to 180°C (a cube of bread will brown in 20 seconds). Fry the eggs until golden brown. Transfer to a baking tray lined with baking paper and bake for 5 minutes to cook through. Remove from the oven and let the eggs rest for a few minutes before cutting in half.

7   Meanwhile, heat a char-grill pan over high heat. Coat the salad onion in the olive oil and season with salt and pepper. Char-grill the onion for 2 minutes each side, until lightly charred.

8   Drain the mushrooms. Serve the eggs with the mushrooms and onion, garnished with micro-coriander, and with Japanese mayonnaise alongside.

The Chiswick Kitchen Garden

There is a push these days for using locally grown produce and nowhere is it more evident than in the restaurant game, with chefs taking great pride in providing customers with the greatest variety of super-fresh ingredients, often grown on site.

Those restaurants that don't have their own garden often contract farmers to grow produce especially for them (we do this at ARIA). When I was setting up my restaurant Chiswick, we were fortunate to have enough space to create a kitchen garden out the back, and I loved the process of turning this into a productive and attractive garden. While it can't supply enough produce for everything we serve at the restaurant, it does create the theme for the menu. The emphasis is on allowing produce to speak for itself; treating it with delicacy and respect to highlight its inherent flavour and freshness. Our approach is simple and natural, and it's continually evolving.

Our garden at Chiswick
is designed to be a feast
for the eyes as well
as the table.

Our gardener at Chiswick,
Peter Hatfield, does an excellent job
keeping it productive and beautiful.

THE CHISWICK KITCHEN GARDEN

Edible flowers are another gift from the garden - nasturtiums, dill, zucchini, thyme...

The garden at Chiswick really helps us stay in touch with the seasons and we cook according to what's at its peak. We've had bumper crops of radishes, lettuce coming out our ears, basil threatening to take over the whole garden bed, and chillies and tomatoes in abundance. Coming up with lots of different ways to use them is a great challenge, and I love knowing our dishes are based on ingredients that are absolutely in their prime. ▪

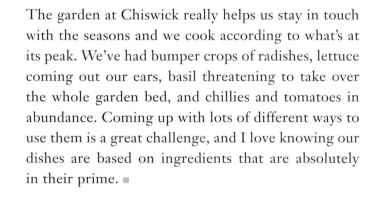

2

Small Plates

Serving a selection of small plates is a great way to feed a larger group; your guests can help themselves to a little bit of everything and enjoy a diverse range of flavours and textures.

100 g sourdough bread

⅔ cup (160 ml) extra virgin olive oil

salt and pepper

juice of 1 lemon

8 red bull's horn peppers

16 giant green kalamata olives

24 marinated white anchovies

oregano leaves, to garnish

Roasted bull's horn peppers with olives and white anchovies

I just can't resist the salty kick of anchovies – they're one of my favourite ingredients and my kids have been eating them since they were babies. Combining them with salty olives, sweet grilled peppers and crisp breadcrumbs is my idea of heaven. Any type of peppers or capsicum will work here.

Serves 4

1   Preheat the oven to 160°C.

2   Tear the sourdough into bite-sized pieces and place on a baking tray. Toss through half the olive oil and season with a bit of salt and pepper. Bake for 10–15 minutes, until crisp. Remove and set aside to cool.

3   Mix the remaining oil with the lemon juice. Set aside.

4   Place the bull's horn peppers, a few at a time, over an open flame or under a hot grill and use tongs to rotate every now and then until the skins are blistered all over. Place in a bowl as you go, covering with plastic film (this makes it easier to remove the skins). Leave for 10–15 minutes, then peel away the skins.

5   Cut the peppers in half, remove the seeds and then quarter. Divide among serving plates. Slice 3 cheeks off each olive and arrange on top of the peppers with the anchovies, croutons and oregano leaves. Season with salt and pepper and drizzle with the lemon dressing.

½ telegraph (long) cucumber

4 red radishes (such as French breakfast), trimmed

1 bunch chives, finely chopped

finely grated zest and juice of 1 lemon

salt and pepper

80 g mayonnaise (see page 211)

2 baby beetroot, trimmed

320 g sashimi-grade kingfish loin

baby beetroot leaves, to garnish

extra virgin olive oil, to drizzle

Kingfish sashimi with radishes and chive aioli

This is one of those great dishes that's really simple and effective. The radishes give a lovely touch of heat and spiciness. You need to use sashimi-grade kingfish for this dish – it's a must when you're serving fish raw.

Serves 4

1 Peel the cucumber, cut in half lengthways and use a teaspoon to scoop out the seeds and discard. Finely dice the cucumber and half the radishes, and put into a small bowl. Add half each of the chives and lemon juice, and season with salt and pepper. Set aside.

2 Combine the mayonnaise, remaining chives and lemon juice, and the lemon zest in a small bowl.

3 Use a mandoline or sharp knife to cut the beetroot and remaining radishes into paper-thin slices.

4 Trim the kingfish, then cut into thin slices and arrange on serving plates. Place a few spoonfuls of the cucumber and radish mixture on and around the fish, then add a few drops of the chive mayonnaise. Add the slices of beetroot and radish, and the beetroot leaves. Finish with a drizzle of extra virgin olive oil.

12 baby (Dutch) carrots, trimmed and scrubbed

pickling liquid (see page 208), to cover

2 teaspoons olive oil

50 g smoked blanched almonds, halved

½ lemon, segmented and diced

2½ tablespoons classic dressing (see page 210)

carrot fronds or parsley leaves, to garnish

Cumin salt

1 teaspoon cumin seeds

½ teaspoon salt flakes

Grilled pickled carrots

Pickling liquid is perfect for carrots, as you get all the extra flavour while still keeping a bit of crunch. If you have a vegie garden, plant some heritage carrots – there are lots of wonderful varieties it can be hard to find unless you grow them yourself.

Serves 4

1 Place the carrots in a heatproof bowl (if you have purple carrots they need to go in a separate bowl as the colour may bleed a little). Pour enough hot pickling liquid over the carrots to cover. Cover the bowl with plastic film and set aside until the carrots and liquid have cooled.

2 To make the cumin salt, toast the cumin seeds in a small dry frying pan over medium heat until aromatic. Transfer to a mortar, add the salt and pound with the pestle until fine and well combined.

3 Preheat a char-grill pan over high heat.

4 Drain the carrots and cut in half lengthways (or into quarters if large). Place in a large bowl, toss through the olive oil and char-grill for 30 seconds each side or until lightly charred. Arrange on serving plates and season with the cumin salt.

5 Combine the smoked almonds, diced lemon and classic dressing in a small bowl. Drizzle over the carrots and garnish with the carrot fronds or parsley.

½ telegraph (long) cucumber, peeled

pickling liquid, to cover (see page 208)

½ avocado, stone removed

juice of ½ lemon

2 teaspoons sugar syrup (see page 211)

1 teaspoon olive oil

pinch of wasabi powder

salt, to taste

320 g sashimi-grade tuna loin

100 g bought seaweed (wakame) salad

micro-coriander or young coriander leaves, to garnish

Salt-cured tuna

There is nothing complicated about this dish, but I guarantee it'll knock the socks off anyone you serve it to. Salt blocks are literally blocks of compressed salt and are available from specialty food stores. They subtly flavour food and also make a great presentation – I am a big fan! Wakame is a bright-green seaweed that's used to make the seaweed salad sold in little plastic containers at most Japanese sushi shops.

Serves 4

1   Cut the cucumber in half lengthways and use a teaspoon to scrape out the seeds. Cut into bite-sized pieces, then place in a heatproof bowl and pour over enough hot pickling liquid to cover. Cover with plastic film and set aside for 30 minutes, then drain well.

2   Scoop the avocado flesh into a blender. Add the lemon juice, sugar syrup and olive oil and blend until smooth. Season with the wasabi and salt, to taste.

3   Trim the tuna and cut into 2.5 cm cubes. Arrange on each salt block with the pickled cucumber, seaweed salad and avocado puree. Garnish with the micro-coriander and serve.

360 g beef fillet, trimmed

1 tablespoon finely chopped cornichons

1 tablespoon finely chopped pickled capers

1 tablespoon finely chopped golden shallot

salt and pepper

4 egg yolks

cornichons, to serve

Tartare relish

100 g tomato sauce (ketchup)

1 tablespoon ginger and shallot sauce (see page 210)

1 teaspoon Tabasco sauce

1 tablespoon Worcestershire sauce

Pommes gaufrettes

2 sebago potatoes, peeled and washed

vegetable oil, for deep-frying

table salt

Steak tartare

This has got the lot – the acidity of cornichons to balance the richness of the meat and egg yolk, the crunch and salt of pommes gaufrettes to contrast the silky smooth tartare. If you don't have a crinkle-cutter attachment for your mandoline, just use the regular blade to thinly slice the potatoes instead.

Serves 4

1 To make the tartare relish, mix all the ingredients in a small bowl until well combined. Set aside.

2 For the pommes gaufrettes, fit the crinkle-cutter attachment on a Japanese mandoline. To slice the potatoes, make one slice and then turn the potato about 90 degrees to the right. Make another slice, then turn back to the start position – this will give the slices a lattice effect. Slice both potatoes this way to make wafer-style chips. (Make sure you use the guard as mandoline blades are dangerously sharp.) Place the chips in cold water so they don't go brown, then drain and pat dry with paper towel when ready to cook.

3 Preheat a deep-fryer to 140°C, or half-fill a large heavy-based saucepan with vegetable oil and heat over medium–high heat to 140°C (a cube of bread will brown in 50 seconds). Add the potato slices, in batches if necessary to avoid crowding the pan, and gently fry for 4–5 minutes or until golden and crisp. Transfer to paper towel to drain and season with the table salt.

4 Use a large sharp knife to finely dice the beef. Combine the beef, cornichons, capers, shallot and tartare relish in a mixing bowl and season with salt and pepper, to taste.

5 Divide the tartare mixture among four small bowls or fill a round mould with a quarter of the mixture at a time and invert onto each serving plate. Place a yolk in the centre of each steak tartare. Serve with the pommes gaufrettes and cornichons alongside.

20 gow gee wrappers

200 ml extra virgin olive oil

70 ml chardonnay vinegar

1 hard-boiled egg, yolk discarded, white finely chopped

1 tablespoon thinly sliced cornichons

1 tablespoon pickled capers, roughly chopped

½ bunch flat-leaf parsley, leaves picked and roughly chopped

Veal braise

2 tablespoons vegetable oil

½ onion, roughly chopped

½ carrot, roughly chopped

½ stalk celery, roughly chopped

½ leek, white part only, washed and roughly chopped

500 g veal shin, trimmed

salt and pepper

1 litre master stock (see page 207)

1 clove garlic, peeled

5 sprigs thyme

2 bay leaves

Veal ravioli

I remember seeing an Asian chef make ravioli using gow gee wrappers many years ago – it's such a simple, foolproof way to do it and is now how I cheat at home. This veal braise is wonderfully rich, so the capers and cornichons are important to give balance. Gherkins would also do the job.

Serves 4

1   To make the veal braise, preheat the oven to 150°C.

2   Heat half the vegetable oil in a flameproof casserole dish over medium–high heat. Add the onion and carrot and cook until they just start to colour, then add the celery and leek and cook until beginning to colour. Take off the heat.

3   Season the veal all over with salt and pepper. Heat the remaining oil in a large heavy-based frying pan over high heat and cook the veal until golden brown. Add to the casserole dish with the master stock (top up with water if necessary to ensure the veal is submerged), garlic and herbs and bring to the boil. Skim off any impurities, then cover and bake for 3 hours or until the meat shreds easily when tested with a fork. Remove from the oven and leave to rest for 30 minutes. Take the meat out of the stock and strain the stock through a fine-meshed sieve into a bowl, reserving the vegetables and discarding the herbs. Reduce 100 ml of the stock in a small saucepan over high heat until it becomes a glaze (once cooled, keep the remaining stock in the fridge for another use).

4   Finely shred the veal into a bowl. Use a blender to blend the reserved vegetables, then add to the veal with the reduced stock and mix well. Taste and season with salt and pepper, if required.

5   Lay the gow gee wrappers on a lightly floured benchtop and place a tablespoon of veal braise in the centre of each. Run a slightly wet finger around the outside edge of a wrapper and fold in half, to make a semicircle. Squeeze any air out and seal the edges by running your fingers all around them and lightly squeezing. Repeat with all the wrappers and filling.

6   Put the remaining ingredients into a small bowl and mix well.

7   Bring a large saucepan of water to the boil over high heat and gently add the ravioli. Boil for 3–4 minutes or until they all float to the surface. Scoop out the ravioli with a slotted spoon. Arrange the ravioli on serving plates, dress with the cornichon and caper mixture, and serve.

16 scallops (without roe)

tarragon leaves, to garnish

shredded parmesan, to garnish

Jerusalem artichoke puree

100 g Jerusalem artichokes, peeled

salt

1 teaspoon salted butter

2 teaspoons pouring cream

Burnt butter

50 g salted butter

2 teaspoons dashi flakes

2 teaspoons rice wine vinegar

Char-grilled scallops with Jerusalem artichoke puree

Scallops are such a sublime ingredient that they're best paired with simple flavour combinations. Here, we have the beautiful earthiness of Jerusalem artichokes with tarragon, and dashi and rice wine vinegar to lift the burnt butter. Look for plump, dry scallops that are still on the shell.

Serves 4

1 To make the Jerusalem artichoke puree, put the Jerusalem artichokes into a heavy-based saucepan and cover with cold water. Season the water with salt, then bring to the boil over medium–high heat. Boil the artichokes for 5 minutes, until tender, then drain. Blend the artichokes in a blender, adding the butter and cream while the motor is running. Blend until smooth, then press through a fine-meshed sieve into a bowl. Cover to keep warm.

2 To make the burnt butter, melt the butter in a small saucepan over medium–high heat. When it begins to turn a light golden brown add the dashi, then finish with the vinegar. Remove from the heat.

3 Heat a char-grill pan over medium heat. Char-grill the scallops for 1–2 minutes each side, until golden and cooked through. Spoon the Jerusalem artichoke puree onto serving plates and add the scallops. Drizzle over the burnt butter, garnish with the tarragon leaves and shredded parmesan, and serve.

4 chicken marylands (leg and thigh portions)

4 chicken wings

2 cloves garlic, finely chopped

1 tablespoon table salt

½ bunch thyme

300 ml buttermilk

vegetable oil, for deep-frying

¼ white cabbage, cored and shredded

¼ bunch chives, finely chopped

1 spring onion, trimmed and thinly sliced

¼ bunch dill, finely chopped

⅓ cup (80 ml) classic dressing (see page 210)

Harissa mayonnaise

⅓ cup (100 g) mayonnaise (see page 211)

1 tablespoon harissa, or to taste

Spiced flour

2 cups (300 g) plain flour

2 teaspoons celery salt

2 teaspoons cayenne pepper

2 teaspoons onion powder

2 teaspoons ground allspice

Crispy buttermilk chicken with harissa mayonnaise

How can you beat fried chicken? This is a classic southern American dish, and it's one of my favourites at Chiswick. The buttermilk tenderises the chicken and it gives it a lovely, delicate flavour – you can pan-fry it in oil instead of deep-frying, if you prefer.

Serves 6–8

1   Using a sharp knife, cut the marylands at each joint to separate the thighs and drumsticks. Place in a large heavy-based saucepan or stockpot. Cut the wings at each joint to separate the winglets, drumettes and wing tips. Discard the wing tips and add the winglets and drumettes to the pan with enough water to cover all the chicken. Add the garlic, salt and thyme and bring to a simmer over medium heat. Gently simmer for 10–15 minutes or until the chicken is cooked through. Take off the heat and let the chicken cool in the liquid, about 30 minutes.

2   Meanwhile, to make the harissa mayonnaise, put the mayonnaise and most of the harissa into a small bowl and whisk until combined. Transfer to a serving bowl, swirl over the remaining harissa, then cover and put into the fridge until ready to serve.

3   To make the spiced flour, combine all the ingredients in a bowl. Set aside.

4   Remove the chicken from the stock (strain the stock and keep for another use). Place the buttermilk in a bowl. Coat each piece of chicken in the buttermilk, then toss in the spiced flour to lightly dust.

5   Preheat a deep-fryer to 180°C, or half-fill a large heavy-based saucepan with vegetable oil and heat over medium–high heat to 180°C (a cube of bread will brown in 20 seconds). Add the chicken, in batches if necessary to avoid crowding the pan, and fry for 3–4 minutes, until golden brown. Use a slotted spoon to transfer the chicken to paper towel to drain.

6   Combine the cabbage, chives, spring onion and dill in a bowl, then toss through the classic dressing. Serve with the chicken and harissa mayonnaise.

400 g sashimi-grade salmon fillets, skin removed

½ telegraph (long) cucumber

½ apple

finely grated zest and juice of ½ lemon

¼ bunch dill, chopped

small bunch watercress, leaves picked

extra virgin olive oil, to garnish

Miso dressing

55 g white miso paste

2 tablespoons grapeseed oil

1½ tablespoons rice wine vinegar

2 teaspoons sugar syrup (see page 211)

1 teaspoon soy sauce

½ clove garlic, finely grated

Croutons

¼ loaf Turkish bread, thinly sliced

olive oil, to drizzle

salt, to sprinkle

Salmon tartare

Miso paste goes really well with seafood – you're in for a treat if you haven't put these two together before. This is light and fresh, with plenty of flavour and crunch, just the ticket for a hot summer's day.

Serves 4

1   To make the miso dressing, whisk all the ingredients together in a small bowl until emulsified.

2   To make the croutons, preheat the oven to 180°C. Spread the bread slices in a single layer over a baking tray. Drizzle with olive oil, sprinkle with salt and bake for 5–8 minutes or until light golden and crisp. Remove and set aside to cool.

3   Use a sharp knife to trim the salmon and cut into 1 cm dice. Place in a medium bowl. Cut the cucumber in half lengthways and use a teaspoon to scrape out the seeds. Dice and add to the bowl. Peel, core and dice the apple, then add to the bowl and toss to combine. Add the lemon zest and juice, dill and 2 tablespoons of the miso dressing and mix well. Divide the tartare mixture among serving plates. Scatter with the watercress and sprinkle with the olive oil. Serve with the remaining miso dressing and the croutons alongside.

4 baby golden beetroot, trimmed

4 baby red beetroot, trimmed

pickling liquid, to cover (see page 208)

100 g jamon, thinly sliced

parsley leaves, to garnish

extra virgin olive oil, to garnish

Celeriac remoulade

200 g celeriac

1½ tablespoons chardonnay vinegar

1 teaspoon salt

2 tablespoons mayonnaise (see page 211)

¼ bunch flat-leaf parsley, finely chopped

salt and pepper

Caramelised walnuts

40 g walnut halves

1 tablespoon icing sugar mixture

Jamon with celeriac remoulade and pickled beetroot

Use jamon iberico from Spain if you can for this dish – it comes from a rare breed of black pig fed on acorns and herbs, and in my eyes it's one of the kings of food. Two varieties of beetroot works beautifully here, so try to get hold of both golden and red (regular) beetroot. You can substitute any other nuts for the walnuts, too.

Serves 4

1   Place the golden beetroot and red beetroot in separate saucepans. Add enough pickling liquid to each pan to cover the beetroot and bring both pans to the boil over medium–high heat. Boil for 15–20 minutes or until a skewer is easily inserted into the centre of the beetroot. Take off the heat and let the beetroot cool in the liquid for 30 minutes. Drain and peel away the skins, then cut 3 beetroot of each colour into quarters and use a mandoline to thinly slice the remaining 2 beetroot.

2   To make the celeriac remoulade, peel the celeriac and thinly slice, then cut the slices into thin strips. Place in a glass or ceramic bowl with the vinegar and salt and leave to marinate for 10 minutes. Drain the celeriac and rinse in cold water, then gently squeeze out any excess water. Place the celeriac in a bowl and mix in the mayonnaise and parsley. Season with salt and pepper, to taste.

3   To make the caramelised walnuts, heat the walnuts in a dry non-stick frying pan over medium heat until lightly toasted and aromatic. Sift a little icing sugar over the nuts and toss gently to coat. Continue sifting the icing sugar over the nuts, a little at a time, tossing constantly, until the icing sugar begins to caramelise, about 4–5 minutes. Sprinkle 1 tablespoon water over the nuts and toss for 30 seconds to finish. Transfer to a baking tray to cool.

4   Place the celeriac remoulade on serving plates and arrange the jamon, beetroot and walnuts around. Garnish with parsley leaves and finish with a drizzle of the extra virgin olive oil.

1 nashi pear

juice of ½ lime

320 g sashimi-grade kingfish loin, skin removed and trimmed

salt and pepper

2½ tablespoons vegetable oil

1 avocado

2 red radishes, trimmed and thinly sliced

flat-leaf parsley leaves, to garnish

extra virgin olive oil, to drizzle

Vodka gel

200 ml vodka

¼ cup (60 ml) sugar syrup (see page 211)

finely grated zest and juice of ¼ orange

finely grated zest and juice of ¼ lemon

finely grated zest and juice of ¼ lime

4 g agar agar

Wasabi salt

1 teaspoon dried wakame seaweed

1 tablespoon salt flakes

½ teaspoon wasabi powder

Seared kingfish with radish, avocado and wasabi

I really love the textural elements in this dish – the softness of the avocado, the firmness of the kingfish, the crunch of the nashi and radish. There's a beautiful balance. A word of advice – make sure you flambé the vodka long enough to burn out the alcohol or the flavour will be too dominant. You can find dried wakame and agar agar at Asian supermarkets and some health food shops.

Serves 4

1   To make the vodka gel, bring the vodka to the boil in a small heavy-based saucepan over high heat. Flambé the vodka – that is, set it alight to burn off the alcohol. When the flame goes out, add the sugar syrup and bring to a simmer. Remove from the heat. Add all the zest and juices and set aside for 5 minutes to infuse, then strain through a fine-meshed sieve and return to the pan. Whisk in the agar agar. Bring to the boil over medium heat, whisking constantly. Boil, still whisking, for 1 minute, then pour into a small bowl. Cover with plastic film and place in the fridge to set, about 20–30 minutes. Once set and cooled, place in a blender and blend to a puree consistency. You may need to add a little water to help blend the gel.

2   Meanwhile, to make the wasabi salt, preheat the oven to 100°C. Pound the wakame in a mortar with a pestle to make small pieces. Place in a bowl with the salt and wasabi. Slowly add 2 teaspoons water, just enough to help stick the wasabi and salt together. Spread the salt mixture over a non-stick baking tray and put into the oven to dry out, about 15 minutes. Remove and cool, then use a mortar and pestle to finely crush. Transfer to a bowl and set aside.

3   Meanwhile, peel the nashi pear, cut into quarters and remove the core, then cut each piece in half again. Place in a small mixing bowl, squeeze over the lime juice and mix well. Set aside for 10 minutes.

4   Place a non-stick heavy-based frying pan over high heat. Season the kingfish with salt and pepper and roll in the vegetable oil, then carefully place in the frying pan and quickly turn so that it is sealed on all sides but still raw in the centre. Place the fish on a plate in the fridge to cool.

5   Cut the avocado in half, remove the stone and peel away the skin without damaging the flesh. Cut each avocado half into quarters. Roll the skinned side of each piece of avocado in the wasabi salt and place on serving plates with the nashi pear. Use a sharp knife to thinly slice the kingfish and add to the plates with the radish. Scatter over a few drops of the vodka gel, garnish with the parsley and finish with a drizzle of the olive oil.

200 g cod fillet, pin-boned, skin removed and cut into chunks

100 g table salt

6 thyme sprigs

½ teaspoon cumin seeds

½ teaspoon coriander seeds

½ teaspoon fennel seeds

2 cups (500 ml) milk

2 cloves garlic, peeled

½ bunch thyme, extra

1 sprig rosemary

1 large potato, peeled and quartered

½ bunch chives, finely chopped

1 teaspoon truffle oil

2 tablespoons shredded parmesan

500 g spiced tomato sauce (see page 209)

micro-coriander or young coriander leaves, to garnish

Polenta chips

100 g instant polenta

60 g butter

60 g parmesan, finely grated

8 sprigs sage, leaves finely chopped

8 sprigs oregano, leaves finely chopped

8 sprigs flat-leaf parsley, finely chopped

½ cup (75 g) plain flour

vegetable oil, for deep-frying

Baked cod brandade with polenta chips

This is a comforting and warming wintry dish. Here, we roll the cod brandade into balls and then grill them in a spicy tomato sauce, but you can also serve it simply as a dip. You could serve the polenta chips as a snack or side dish for a main course, too.

Serves 4

1   Put the fish into a glass or ceramic dish. Combine the salt, thyme and spices and mix into the fish, then cover with plastic film and put into the fridge for 30 minutes. Wash the fish thoroughly and pat dry with paper towel, then put into a heavy-based saucepan with the milk, garlic, extra thyme and the rosemary and bring to the boil. Remove from the heat and set aside for 15 minutes, then take out the fish and flake it into a bowl.

2   Meanwhile, to make the polenta chips, bring 400 ml water to a rapid boil in a heavy-based saucepan over high heat. Add the polenta in a slow steady stream, reduce the heat to low and whisk until thickened, about 5 minutes. Add the butter and parmesan and whisk for 5 minutes more. Whisk in the herbs. Sprinkle a 30 cm × 20 cm roasting pan with a little water, then pour in the polenta and smooth the surface. Cover with baking paper and place in the fridge for 2 hours to set. Once set, remove and cut into 6 cm × 2 cm batons, then toss in the flour.

3   Place the potato in a heavy-based saucepan and cover with cold water. Bring to the boil over high heat and boil until tender. Drain, then press through a potato ricer or use a potato masher to mash well. Add to the flaked fish with the chives, truffle oil and half the parmesan and gently mix together. Taste and adjust the seasoning, if required. Roll the mixture into small balls (about the size of a golf ball).

4   Preheat the oven to 200°C.

5   Spread the spiced tomato sauce over a large, shallow ovenproof dish or 4 smaller dishes, add the brandade balls and sprinkle over the remaining parmesan. Bake for 10 minutes or until the brandade balls are golden.

6   Meanwhile, preheat a deep-fryer to 180°C, or half-fill a large heavy-based saucepan with vegetable oil and heat over medium–high heat to 180°C (a cube of bread will brown in 20 seconds). Fry the polenta chips, in batches if necessary, for 1–2 minutes or until golden. Transfer to paper towel to drain.

7   Serve the baked cod brandade garnished with the micro-coriander and with the polenta chips alongside.

vegetable oil, for deep-frying

28 raw medium-sized prawns, peeled and deveined, halved

30 g plain flour

table salt

½ iceberg lettuce

2½ tablespoons classic dressing (see page 210)

1 lemon, quartered

1 pickled jalapeño (see page 200), sliced

2 pickled red chillies (see page 198), sliced

Beer batter

270 g self-raising flour

1 teaspoon salt

1 teaspoon ground white pepper

170 ml beer

Jalapeño mayonnaise

½ pickled jalapeño (see page 200)

pinch of hot chilli powder

2 teaspoons sugar syrup (see page 211)

⅓ cup (100 g) mayonnaise (see page 211)

Popcorn prawns with jalapeño mayonnaise

These tasty little morsels are a real crowd-pleaser. Make sure your oil is at the right temperature before adding the prawns so the batter is nice and crisp. Jalapeño sweetened in sugar syrup gives a lovely kick to the mayonnaise.

Serves 6

1   To make the beer batter, combine the flour, salt and pepper in a bowl. Whisk in 300 ml water until there are no lumps, then whisk in the beer. Cover with plastic film and set aside for 30 minutes.

2   For the jalapeño mayonnaise, place the jalapeño, chilli powder and sugar syrup in a small food processor or the chopper bowl of a stick mixer and process to a smooth paste. Add about a quarter of the mayonnaise and blend for 30 seconds, then transfer to a bowl and whisk through the rest of the mayonnaise. Set aside.

3   Preheat a deep-fryer to 180°C, or half-fill a large heavy-based saucepan with vegetable oil and heat over medium–high heat to 180°C (a cube of bread will brown in 20 seconds). Toss the prawn halves in the flour to coat, then dip in the beer batter and let the excess batter drip off. Gently lower into the hot oil and fry for 4–5 minutes, until golden, then transfer to paper towel to drain and season with table salt. (You may need to fry the prawns in batches, depending on the size of your pan.)

4   Cut the lettuce into wedges, toss with the classic dressing and place in serving bowls. Add the prawns and lemon wedges. Scatter over all the pickled chilli, and serve with the jalapeño mayonnaise on the side.

4 kipfler potatoes, scrubbed

2 teaspoons olive oil

good pinch of sweet paprika

40 g pitted large green olives, quartered

2 tablespoons pine nuts, toasted

40 g marinated white anchovies

micro-parsley or young flat-leaf parsley leaves, to garnish

Braised octopus

500 g cleaned baby octopus

¼ bunch flat-leaf parsley, stems only (reserve the leaves for garnish)

¼ bunch thyme

finely grated zest of 1 lemon

3 cloves garlic, crushed

2 bay leaves

1 tablespoon salt

1 teaspoon white peppercorns

Lemon and muscat vinegar dressing

1 lemon

3 teaspoons verjuice

3 teaspoons muscat vinegar

100 ml olive oil

¼ bunch thyme, leaves chopped

Braised octopus with anchovies, potatoes and olives

Braising is a great cooking method for octopus – it tenderises and imparts flavour, so it's a win-win. Muscat vinegar is made from muscat wine and has a beautiful sweet–sour flavour. You can find it at specialty food stores.

Serves 4

1   To make the braised octopus, place all the ingredients in a large heavy-based saucepan. Add enough water to cover the octopus and bring to a gentle simmer over medium heat. Simmer for 1 hour or until the octopus is tender. Drain the octopus and set aside to cool; discard the solids.

2   To make the lemon and muscat vinegar dressing, finely grate the zest from the lemon into a bowl. Remove the pith from the lemon, cut the flesh into segments and roughly chop. Add to the bowl with the verjuice and vinegar, then whisk in the olive oil until combined. Season with salt and pepper, then stir in the thyme.

3   Place the potatoes in a heavy-based saucepan of cold salted water and bring to a simmer over medium heat. Simmer for 10–15 minutes, until the potatoes are tender when tested with a skewer. Drain well.

4   Meanwhile, heat the olive oil in a non-stick heavy-based frying pan over medium–high heat. Add the octopus, sprinkle with the paprika and pan-fry for 1–2 minutes, until slightly crisp.

5   Cut the potatoes into thick rounds and place on serving plates with the octopus, olives and pine nuts. Drizzle over the dressing and garnish with the anchovies and parsley leaves.

vegetable oil, for shallow-frying

100 g pickled capers

½ bunch sage, leaves picked

table salt and pepper

3 bunches asparagus

⅓ cup (80 ml) olive oil,
plus extra for drizzling

1 tablespoon white vinegar

2 eggs

edible flowers (such as viola), to garnish

Grilled asparagus, fried capers and soft-poached egg

The minute you see new-season asparagus for sale, grab some and make this dish. We serve it on two plates for sharing, but if you'd like to serve it as a starter for four, poach an egg for each plate. Edible flowers are something we particularly like to use at Chiswick restaurant – everything from violas, which pop up between the pavers, to snow pea flowers, which have a really lovely, subtle flavour.

Serves 4

1   Add enough vegetable oil to a deep, heavy-based frying pan to come about 1 cm up the side. Bring to 160°C over medium heat (a cube of bread will brown in 30 seconds). Add the capers and fry for 1 minute or until crisp and translucent. Transfer to paper towel to drain. Using the same hot oil, fry the sage leaves for 30 seconds or until crisp, then drain on paper towel and season with table salt.

2   Preheat a char-grill pan over medium heat.

3   Use a knife to trim the bottom of each asparagus spear. Place the asparagus in a mixing bowl, add the olive oil and toss to coat. Season with salt and pepper and char-grill, in batches if necessary, for 3–4 minutes, turning often, until tender and lightly charred all over. Remove from the pan and arrange into nests on 2 serving plates.

4   Add enough hot water to a heavy-based saucepan to come three-quarters of the way up the side, then add the vinegar and bring to a simmer over low heat. Use a spoon to create a gentle whirlpool effect, then crack each egg into the centre of the whirlpool and cook for 3½ minutes. Use a slotted spoon to transfer the eggs to paper towel to drain. Place an egg in the centre of each asparagus nest and sprinkle over the capers and sage leaves. Garnish with the flowers, a drizzle of olive oil and a sprinkling of salt.

300 g yams, scrubbed

2½ tablespoons olive oil

¼ bunch rosemary, leaves picked

¼ bunch thyme, leaves picked

2 cloves garlic, smashed

salt and pepper

4 pickling onions

100 g butter, softened

100 g woodchips or hickory chips

2 tablespoons soft goat's cheese (chevre)

small handful red-vein sorrel

purple kale leaves, to garnish

1½ tablespoons classic dressing
(see page 210)

Smoked yams, goat's cheese and charred onions

Yams are similar to potatoes, but their flavour is sweeter and has a delicious nutty quality. Roasting and then smoking them gives a really fantastic flavour. They can be hard to find, but it's worth seeking them out. If you don't have any luck, use sweet potato or Jerusalem artichokes instead. You could also serve this as a side dish for roasted meat.

Serves 4

1   Preheat the oven to 180°C.

2   Place the yams in a roasting pan and toss through the olive oil, rosemary, thyme and garlic. Season with salt and pepper and bake for 10–15 minutes or until tender. Remove and transfer the yams to a wire rack.

3   Meanwhile, cut the onions in half through the root, leaving the skin on. Spread the butter over the base of a heavy-based saucepan and season with salt and pepper. Place the onions in the pan, cut-side down, and press into the butter. Add 200 ml water or enough to come halfway up the sides of the onions. Cover with a cartouche (a round of baking paper) and place over medium heat. Cook for 10–15 minutes, until the water has evaporated, the butter is golden brown and the cut sides of the onions are caramelised. Remove from the heat and set aside for 5 minutes to cool slightly, then peel.

4   Line a baking tray with foil and scatter over the woodchips. Have a large flameproof lid that's big enough to cover the woodchips close at hand. Place the tray on the stovetop and carefully use a kitchen blowtorch to set the chips alight, then cover with the lid to put the fire out. Lift the lid – the chips should be smoking – and place the rack of yams over them. Cover with the lid and leave for 3 minutes. Remove the lid.

5   Place the yams and onions on serving plates, scatter over the goat's cheese, sorrel and purple kale, and finish with a drizzle of classic dressing.

Suppliers

I've been so fortunate during my career to connect with passionate, dedicated suppliers who I can rely on to deliver produce of the very best quality, every time. I couldn't do what I do without them.

I love talking to Tony Mann of Export Fresh about new varieties he's trialling.

So much has changed during my cooking career. Everyday produce now comes in countless varieties, and many ingredients I had never heard of twenty years ago are not only widely available, but can often be picked up at the local shops. Food has come a long, long way. There has been an explosion of cooking and food-based travel shows on television that have generated mass appeal, and people are attempting to cook everything from sophisticated high-end dishes to traditional home-style fare themselves. The world is becoming a smaller place, too, so chefs are travelling more than they used to, bringing back new ideas and requesting exotic produce from their suppliers. Who knows where we will be in five years time!

The delicate flavour of micro salad leaves is just one of the many food trends our suppliers have introduced us to.

SUPPLIERS

4 × 200 g beef sirloin steaks

salt and pepper

olive oil, for drizzling

½ bunch chives, finely chopped

1 small fresh horseradish

lemon halves, to serve

Celeriac puree

20 g butter

1 golden shallot, finely diced

½ clove garlic, crushed

1 small celeriac, peeled and diced

finely grated zest of 1 lemon

i tablespoon fresh lemon juice, or to taste

2½ tablespoons pouring cream

2 teaspoons olive oil

salt and pepper

Char-grilled beef sirloin

Dad and I predominantly breed sheep at the family farm, but we've always had a small herd of cattle, too. We like to vary the breed and try new ones as much as possible, the latest being Angus cross Shorthorn. Not surprisingly, we have steak pretty often, at least once a week, and I get cravings for it every now and then. This is how I serve it up for the family.

Serves 4

1   To make the celeriac puree, melt the butter in a heavy-based saucepan over medium heat, then add the shallot and garlic and cook for 3–5 minutes, until softened. Add the celeriac and cook for 5 minutes, then pour in 2½ tablespoons water and cook for a further 8–10 minutes, until the celeriac is tender. Transfer to a blender with the lemon zest and juice and blend to combine. Add the cream and blend to mix in. Continue to blend, slowly adding the olive oil to emulsify. Press through a fine-meshed sieve into a bowl and season with salt and pepper, to taste. Cover to keep warm.

2   Heat a char-grill pan over medium heat. Season the steaks and drizzle over the olive oil. Grill the steaks for 2–3 minutes, until lightly charred, then rotate to create cross-hatched grill marks and cook for a further i minute. Turn over and repeat the process. This will result in rare to medium–rare steaks.

3   Place the steaks on serving plates and sprinkle with chives, then grate over horseradish, to taste. Serve with the celeriac puree and lemon halves.

200 g fresh shelled peas (from about 400 g peas in pods)

ice cubes

1 litre chicken stock (see page 206)

80 g butter

2 golden shallots, finely diced

2 cloves garlic, finely chopped

⅔ cup (160 ml) white wine

2½ cups (500 g) arborio rice

400 g raw spanner crabmeat

120 g crème fraîche

50 g finely grated parmesan, plus extra to serve

½ bunch chives, finely chopped

small handful tarragon leaves

small handful flat-leaf parsley leaves

juice of 1 lemon

salt and pepper

Crab and pea risotto

I have one condition for making this risotto and it's non-negotiable – you must use good-quality fresh crabmeat. I was introduced to spanner crab when I opened ARIA Brisbane and was blown away by its incredibly sweet, firm flesh. I was actually bitten by one on live TV once, but I got my revenge by cooking him up that night! Adding crème fraîche at the end gives a lovely richness and mild acidity.

Serves 4

1 Cook the peas in a saucepan of boiling salted water for 2–3 minutes, until tender. Remove and refresh in a bowl of iced water.

2 Bring the stock to the boil in a small heavy-based saucepan over high heat, then reduce the heat to keep it at a simmer. Melt the butter in a separate heavy-based saucepan over medium heat and cook the shallot and garlic for 3–4 minutes, until softened. Add the wine and cook until reduced to a glaze, then add the rice and stir until well coated. Add a ladleful of the hot stock and stir with a wooden spoon until absorbed. Keep adding the stock, one ladleful at a time and waiting until it is absorbed before adding more, until the rice is just al dente.

3 Add the crabmeat and continue stirring for 1–2 minutes, until it changes colour, then add the crème fraîche, parmesan and peas. Finish the risotto by stirring through the herbs, lemon juice and salt and pepper, to taste.

600 g orecchiette

16 spears asparagus, trimmed and quartered

ice cubes

2 cloves garlic

1½ tablespoons olive oil

24 cherry tomatoes, halved

¼ bunch basil, leaves torn, to serve

shaved parmesan, to serve

Basil pesto

½ bunch basil, leaves picked

25 g pine nuts, toasted

½ clove garlic, roughly chopped

150 ml olive oil

50 g finely grated parmesan

Orecchiette with basil pesto and tomatoes

Basil is one of my favourite herbs to grow, and making pesto is my favourite thing to do when the plants are thriving in summer. Chopping and grating ingredients that are going into the food processor may seem like a waste of time, but there's method in the madness. Prolonged friction from the blade will turn the basil black, so you want the processing time to be as brief as possible.

Serves 4–6

1 To make the basil pesto, put the basil, pine nuts and garlic into a food processor and process until finely chopped. With the motor running, slowly add enough of the oil to bind the pesto together. Add the cheese and process for 30 seconds.

2 Cook the pasta in plenty of boiling salted water according to the instructions on the packet, then drain.

3 Blanch the asparagus in a saucepan of boiling salted water for 1–2 minutes, until just tender. Drain and refresh in a bowl of iced water.

4 Use a sharp knife or mandoline to carefully cut the garlic into paper-thin slices.

5 Heat the olive oil in a large heavy-based frying pan over high heat and fry the garlic until golden. Add the asparagus and tomato and saute for 1 minute, then add the pasta and pesto. Cook, tossing, until well combined. Serve scattered with the torn basil leaves and shaved parmesan.

1.2 kg chicken

chicken stock (see page 206), to cover

⅓ cup (100 g) mayonnaise (see page 211)

100 g Greek-style yoghurt

2 teaspoons curry powder

finely grated zest of 1 lime

finely grated zest and juice of ½ lemon

¼ bunch mint, leaves picked

¼ bunch coriander, leaves picked

2 granny smith apples, peeled, cored and cut into matchsticks

100 g roasted cashews

char-grilled sourdough bread, to serve

Mango chutney

1 tablespoon vegetable oil

1 golden shallot, thinly sliced

½ red chilli, seeded and finely chopped

3 tablespoons caster sugar

100 ml chardonnay vinegar

2 mangoes, peeled and seeded, flesh chopped

Coronation chicken

This is my version of the famous dish invented for the coronation banquet of Queen Elizabeth in 1953. It came to my attention thanks to all the English guys who have worked with me over the years and though it may be traditional, it's worth revisiting. If you need to save time, you can use Sharwood's mango chutney instead of making your own.

Serves 4

1   To make the mango chutney, heat the vegetable oil in a small heavy-based saucepan over medium heat. Saute the shallot and chilli for 5 minutes, then add the sugar and cook until it melts and becomes a light caramel. Add the vinegar to deglaze, then add the mango and 2½ tablespoons water and cook over very low heat for 10 minutes, until it reaches a jam-like consistency. Set aside to cool.

2   Place the chicken in a large heavy-based saucepan and cover with the stock. Bring to the boil over medium–high heat, then reduce the heat and simmer for 15 minutes. Remove from the heat and let the chicken cool in the stock – this will take about 1½ hours. Once cooled, take it out of the pan and shred the meat, discarding the skin and bones.

3   Place the chicken in a large bowl with the mango chutney, mayonnaise, yoghurt, curry powder, lime zest, lemon zest and juice, herbs and half each of the apple and crushed cashews. Lightly mix together until well combined. Place the chicken mixture on a serving plate and garnish with the remaining apple and cashews. Serve with the char-grilled sourdough.

⅔ cup (100 g) plain flour

salt and pepper

4 veal osso buco

⅔ cup (160 ml) vegetable oil

2 carrots, cut into 1 cm dice

2 onions, finely diced

2 cloves garlic, finely chopped

¼ stalk celery, cut into 1 cm dice

½ leek, white part only, washed and cut into 1 cm dice

2 oranges

2 cinnamon sticks

2 star anise

pinch of saffron threads

3 cloves

1½ tablespoons harissa

200 ml red wine

100 ml veal stock (see page 207)

500 g tomato sauce (see page 209)

1 tablespoon caster sugar

6 dates, pitted and quartered

¼ bunch coriander, leaves picked

¼ bunch mint, leaves picked

Spiced braised veal shanks with leek, orange and dates

When the weather's cold and wet I like nothing better than grabbing some veal shanks and braising them over the afternoon. Here, I've used classic Middle Eastern flavours: spices, dates, orange and mint, and it would be delicious with couscous. The kids love having the leftovers packed into flasks for their school lunches.

Serves 4

1 Preheat the oven to 160°C.

2 Season the flour with salt and pepper, then add the osso buco and toss to coat. Heat half the vegetable oil in a heavy-based frying pan over medium–high heat and seal the osso buco on each side. Transfer to a bowl and set aside.

3 Heat the remaining oil in a large flameproof casserole dish over medium heat and saute the carrot, onion and garlic for 4–5 minutes, until softened. Add the celery and leek and saute for a further 4 minutes. Use a vegetable peeler to remove the zest from 1 orange in long, wide strips, then juice the orange. Add the zest to the pan with the spices and cook, stirring, for 2 minutes. Stir in the harissa and cook for 2 minutes more. Add the orange juice and red wine, stirring to deglaze. When the liquid has reduced to a glaze, add the osso buco, veal stock, tomato sauce and sugar and bring to a gentle simmer.

4 Cover and bake for 1½ hours, then stir through the dates, cover and bake for a further 30 minutes, until the meat is just starting to come away from the bones.

5 Peel the remaining orange, remove the pith and segment the flesh. Serve the veal shanks sprinkled with the herbs and garnished with orange segments.

4 jumbo quail

8 cloves garlic, smashed

¼ bunch thyme

1 lemon, zest removed in wide strips, juiced

1 orange, zest removed in wide strips, juiced

salt and pepper

2 bulbs baby fennel, tough outer layers removed

2½ tablespoons vegetable oil

2 sprigs rosemary

20 g butter

100 ml red wine

5 candied cumquats (see page 197)

Mustard dressing

2 teaspoons wholegrain mustard

1 teaspoon Dijon mustard

2 teaspoons Champagne vinegar

2 teaspoons honey

½ cup (125 ml) grapeseed oil

salt and pepper

Roasted jumbo quail, candied cumquats and fennel with mustard dressing

We are getting much better at producing game in this country and I like to support the industry. Quail meat is a little bit darker than chicken and has a delicious gamey taste. If you're nervous about trussing it, ask your butcher to do it for you. You could also use spatchcock. The mustard dressing here would go well with other game or meats, particularly veal.

Serves 4

1   Preheat the oven to 180°C.

2   To make the mustard dressing, whisk the mustards, vinegar and honey in a bowl until combined. Slowly add the oil while whisking constantly, until emulsified. Whisk in 1 tablespoon water to thin the dressing, then season with salt and pepper, to taste.

3   Use a sharp knife to trim any excess skin from the quails and cut off the wing tips. Make sure all the internal organs are removed. Place a garlic clove, sprig of thyme and a strip of lemon and orange zest in the cavity of each quail. Truss each quail by passing a long piece of kitchen string underneath the back. Bring the ends of the string up around each leg and cross the ends over the top. Bring the string under the drumsticks and pull both ends to pull the legs together. Draw the ends of the string along either side of the quail and over the wing joints. Turn the quail onto its breast, cross the string over the back and tighten to pull the wings close to the body. Tie the string securely so the quail will keep their shape during cooking. Season generously with salt and pepper.

4   Cut the fennel bulbs into quarters. Heat the vegetable oil in a large ovenproof saucepan or flameproof casserole dish over high heat. Add the fennel and cook for 2–3 minutes or until golden brown. Turn and cook for 1 minute, then add the quail, remaining garlic and the rosemary and cook, turning the quail every now and then, until the quail are golden brown all over. Add the butter and baste the quail, then pour in the lemon and orange juice. Put into the oven and bake for 5 minutes, then return to the stovetop on medium heat and add the wine, stirring to deglaze the pan. Remove from the heat.

5   Serve the quail and fennel drizzled with the pan juices and mustard dressing, and garnished with the cumquats.

4 duck marylands (leg and thigh portions)

salt and pepper

4 cloves garlic, peeled and smashed

4 sprigs thyme

2 sprigs rosemary

2 litres duck fat

500 g Jerusalem artichokes, scrubbed

2 bunches salad onions, stems trimmed, halved

4 sage leaves

2 bay leaves

50 g cornichons, halved

chervil sprigs, to garnish

Salsa verde

1 clove garlic

100 ml olive oil

¼ bunch flat-leaf parsley, leaves picked

¼ bunch basil, leaves picked

¼ bunch mint, leaves picked

1 tablespoon chardonnay vinegar

finely grated zest and juice of 1 lemon

salt and pepper

Confit duck leg with roasted Jerusalem artichokes and onions

I remember having duck confit at Chez L'Ami Louis in Paris and thinking it had to be the best in the world. I've had it many times since then and my opinion hasn't changed, but this is an excellent version for cooking at home. You can find duck fat at delicatessens and gourmet food stores.

Serves 4

1   Preheat the oven to 120°C.

2   Season the duck with salt and pepper and place in a large ovenproof saucepan with 3 cloves of garlic, 2 sprigs of thyme and 1 sprig of rosemary. Add the duck fat and bring to a simmer over medium heat. Place a cartouche (a round of baking paper) over the duck portions to keep them submerged in the fat, then cover and bake for 2 hours, until the meats starts to come away from the bone. Take out of the oven and let the duck rest in the fat. Increase the heat to 180°C.

3   Cut the Jerusalem artichokes into bite-sized pieces, leaving the skin on.

4   Place a large ovenproof frying pan over high heat and add 100 ml of the duck fat from the confit. When it's hot, add the Jerusalem artichokes, onions, the remaining garlic, thyme and rosemary, and the sage. Season with salt and pepper. Cook, shaking the pan occasionally, for 5 minutes. Add the bay leaves, put into the oven and bake for 15–25 minutes, until the artichokes are tender. Return to the stovetop over medium heat. Drain the duck portions from the fat and add to the frying pan, skin-side down. Cook for 2–3 minutes, until the skin on the duck is golden brown and crisp.

5   Meanwhile, to make the salsa verde, place the garlic in a blender with the olive oil and blend until finely chopped. Add the herbs and blend to a smooth, thick paste. Mix in the vinegar and lemon zest and juice. Season with salt and pepper, to taste, then transfer to a serving bowl.

6   Place the duck, artichokes, onions and cornichons on serving plates. Serve scattered with the chervil and with a good spoonful of the salsa verde.

1 bunch baby purple beetroot, trimmed

1 bunch baby golden beetroot, trimmed

pickling liquid, to cover (see page 208)

⅔ cup (100 g) plain flour

1 tablespoon mild paprika

salt

4 blue mackerel, filleted

2½ tablespoons vegetable oil

6 pieces pickled green tomato (see page 200), cut into wedges

1 orange, segmented

handful frisee (curly endive) leaves

¼ bunch dill, leaves picked

handful baby red-vein sorrel

handful picked watercress leaves

Cardamom and orange dressing

1 tablespoon cardamom pods

100 ml classic dressing (see page 210)

finely grated zest of 1 orange

1½ tablespoons fresh orange juice

Blue mackerel with beetroot, cardamom and orange

Mackerel is an oily fish and that's exactly what we want in this dish. It is strong and meaty and goes really well with the beautiful earthy flavour of the beetroot. Ask your fishmonger to fillet the mackerel for you.

Serves 4

1 Set aside a beetroot of each colour and place the rest in two separate saucepans (purple in one, golden in the other). Pour over enough pickling liquid to cover and bring both pans to the boil over medium heat. Boil for 15 minutes or until the beetroot are tender when tested with a skewer. Remove from the heat and set aside until the beetroot and liquid have cooled. Drain the beetroot, peel away the skin and cut into quarters.

2 To make the cardamom and orange dressing, put the cardamom in a mortar and pound with the pestle until lightly crushed. Discard the pods and keep the seeds. Toast the seeds in a small dry frying pan over medium heat until they have released their oils and are aromatic. Combine the cardamom seeds, classic dressing and orange zest and juice in a bowl and whisk well. Set aside for 20 minutes to infuse.

3 Combine the flour and paprika and season with salt. Cut each mackerel fillet in half and lightly dust in the seasoned flour, shaking off any excess. Heat the vegetable oil in a large heavy-based frying pan over medium–high heat, add the fish, skin-side down, and cook for 2–3 minutes or until the skin is golden brown and crisp. Turn and cook for a further 30 seconds or until just cooked through, then remove from the pan.

4 Use a mandoline to thinly slice the reserved purple and golden beetroot.

5 Arrange the pickled beetroot, thinly sliced beetroot, pickled tomato wedges, orange segments, frisee, dill, sorrel and watercress on serving plates. Drizzle over the dressing, add the fish and serve.

1.2 kg chicken

3 litres chicken stock (see page 206)

1 bay leaf

1 sprig thyme

salt and pepper

1 cob sweetcorn, husk and silk removed

½ bunch curly kale, trimmed

2 tablespoons olive oil

½ leek, white part only, washed and chopped

150 g orzo (risoni) or other small pasta

¼ bunch tarragon, leaves picked

Chicken soup

Whenever I feel like I'm coming down with a cold, or just want something light and wholesome to eat, I make this chicken soup. It's satisfying, warms you up and makes you feel better. Truly. I really encourage you to use homemade stock – nothing beats its flavour and freshness.

Serves 4

1   Place the chicken in a heavy-based saucepan and pour over the stock – the chicken should be completely covered (top up with a little water if it isn't). Add the bay leaf and thyme and season lightly with salt and pepper. Bring to a gentle simmer over medium heat, then reduce the heat to hold at a very gentle simmer for 30 minutes. Take off the heat and leave the chicken to cool in the stock for 30 minutes. Remove the chicken (reserve the stock) and shred the meat, discarding the skin and bones. Set aside.

2   While the chicken is cooling, cut the corn kernels from the cob. Tear the kale leaves into bite-sized pieces and roughly chop the stalks. Heat the olive oil in a large heavy-based saucepan over medium heat. Add the leek and kale stalks, season with salt and pepper and cook for 5 minutes or until softened. Add the corn kernels and cook for 2 minutes, then add the kale leaves. Strain the reserved chicken stock and pour over the vegetables, then add the pasta and bring to the boil over high heat. Reduce the heat to low–medium and simmer for 10 minutes. Add the shredded chicken and tarragon, increase the heat to medium–high and return to the boil. Taste and adjust the seasoning, if required. Ladle into serving bowls and serve.

Community Gardens

I can't say enough about the value of community gardens. They embody exactly the kind of community spirit I wish we saw more of. The two we photographed here are typical of all those I've visited - happy, buzzing, productive places.

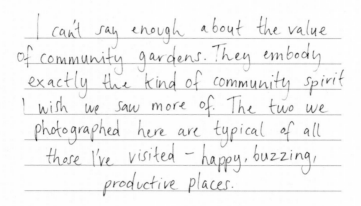

The idea is simple – you don't have space for a kitchen garden at home, so you go to a communal area and dig, plant, water and weed to your heart's content. Everybody pitches in and everybody reaps the benefits – bags and boxes of whatever is ripe for the picking, sure, but much more besides. There's the camaraderie of getting together with other people and doing something productive, and the neighbourly bonds that begin in the garden and extend from there, sometimes leading to lifelong friendships and an invaluable local support network. People from all walks of life and ethnic backgrounds come together, which is important as it introduces varieties of fruit and vegetables that may not otherwise have been available, or perhaps some people have never heard of, which really broadens our horizons. If you don't have space for a kitchen garden at home, or you just want to meet like-minded people and get involved in your community, go and visit one near you.

Zorka Petrovska (left) and Asiye Kartop (right) at the Riverwood Community Garden.

This is the sort of garden I'd like to have at home — they grow everything here, it's like an edible jungle.

COMMUNITY GARDENS

1.2 kg chicken

salt and pepper

⅓ cup (80 ml) olive oil,
plus 2 teaspoons, extra

1 lemon, halved

Spiced hay

large handful organic hay

1 cinnamon stick

1 star anise

½ teaspoon fennel seeds

½ teaspoon coriander seeds

½ teaspoon cumin seeds

½ lemon, zest removed in wide strips

½ orange, zest removed in wide strips

Stuffing

100 g crustless sourdough bread,
torn into pieces

⅓ cup (80 ml) milk

80 g butter

2 golden shallots, finely diced

1 clove garlic, finely chopped

finely grated zest of 1 lemon

¼ bunch rosemary, leaves chopped

¼ bunch thyme, leaves chopped

¼ bunch flat-leaf parsley, leaves chopped

salt and pepper

Hay-roasted chicken

The smell of freshly cut hay takes me back to the farm where I spent most of my childhood. I just love it. Here, it permeates through the chicken giving it the most amazing flavour. You can buy organic hay from pet stores. An alternative would be to use hardy herbs – you won't get the same aromatics, but you will still get a lovely flavour. A salad using iceberg lettuce, such as the one on page 140, would be a great accompaniment.

Serves 4

1   Preheat the oven to 220°C.

2   For the spiced hay, combine all the ingredients in a mixing bowl. Line a roasting pan with foil. Place the hay mixture in the pan and set a wire rack over the top.

3   To make the stuffing, soak the bread in the milk for 5 minutes or until softened, then remove and squeeze out any excess milk. Melt the butter in a small frying pan over medium heat and cook the shallot and garlic for 3–4 minutes, until softened. Transfer to a food processor with the remaining ingredients and process until combined, but still a little chunky. Season with salt and pepper and set aside to cool completely.

4   Use a sharp knife to remove the wishbone from the chicken and trim any excess skin or fat. Fill the cavity of the chicken with the cooled stuffing. Use kitchen string to truss the chicken so it holds its shape during cooking and the stuffing doesn't fall out. Season with salt and pepper and rub the olive oil over the skin.

5   Place the chicken on the wire rack over the hay and roast for 20 minutes, until the skin starts to turn golden brown. Reduce the oven temperature to 180°C and roast for a further 40 minutes or until the juices run clear when the leg joint is pierced with a skewer. Take out of the oven and let the chicken rest for 5 minutes.

6   While the chicken is resting, heat the extra olive oil in a small heavy-based frying pan over high heat. Add the lemon halves, cut side down, and cook for 3–5 minutes, until caramelised. Serve the chicken with the lemon.

⅓ cup (80 ml) vegetable oil

1 onion, finely diced

1 clove garlic, finely chopped

2 teaspoons ground cumin

2 teaspoons ground coriander

2 tablespoons harissa

1 tablespoon tomato paste

⅓ cup (80 ml) white wine

⅓ cup (80 ml) chardonnay vinegar

800 g tomato sauce (see page 209)

2 sprigs coriander, leaves picked, stems and roots finely chopped

salt and pepper

juice of 1 lemon

650 g cod fillets, pin-boned and skin removed, diced

8 raw medium–large prawns, peeled and deveined

30 g butter, diced

micro-coriander or small coriander leaves, to garnish

Saffron couscous

pinch of saffron threads

½ cup (100 g) couscous

1 tablespoon olive oil

2 pieces preserved lemon, rind only, rinsed and finely diced (see page 194)

salt and pepper

Seafood tagine with saffron couscous

This tagine is a little different in that it's upside-down to the way it's usually served. Having the couscous crust on the top is brilliant, as it gives a slight crunch and also soaks up all the delicious flavours from below.

Serves 4

1 Heat the vegetable oil in a large heavy-based saucepan over medium heat and cook the onion and garlic for 3–4 minutes, until softened. Add the spices, harissa and tomato paste and cook, stirring constantly, for 2 minutes or until aromatic. Add the wine and vinegar and cook, stirring to deglaze the pan. Add the tomato sauce and chopped coriander stems and roots, and cook over low–medium heat for 30–45 minutes, until thickened slightly. Season with salt and pepper, to taste, and stir in the lemon juice. Set aside.

2 Meanwhile, to make the saffron couscous, put ½ cup (125 ml) water and the saffron into a small saucepan and bring to the boil. Place the couscous in a heatproof bowl and toss through the olive oil. Pour the boiling water over the couscous, cover with plastic film and give a good shake, then set aside while the couscous absorbs the liquid. Use a spoon to gently stir the couscous to separate the grains. Add the preserved lemon and stir to combine. Season with salt and pepper, to taste.

3 Preheat the oven to 180°C.

4 Place the cod in a tagine dish or casserole dish. Cover with the tomato mixture, place the prawns on top, cover with a cartouche (a round of baking paper) and bake for 8–10 minutes or until the fish is cooked through. Roughly chop the coriander leaves and stir through. Spoon the couscous over the tagine, dot with the butter and return to the oven for 2–4 minutes, until the butter has melted and the couscous is warm. Garnish with coriander and serve.

50 g speck, thinly sliced

8 small pickling onions

ice cubes

1 tablespoon olive oil

20 g butter

2 tablespoons sherry vinegar

70 g cavolo nero (Tuscan kale), trimmed and torn

200 ml milk

200 g sour cream

6 eggs, beaten lightly

pinch of cayenne pepper

pinch of salt, or to taste

Shortcrust pastry

1⅓ cups (200 g) plain flour, plus extra for dusting

pinch of salt

100 g unsalted butter, chilled and diced

1 egg

Caramelised onion, speck and cavolo nero tart

When I started out in the food industry I wanted to be a baker or pastry chef, because I liked the idea of finishing work at midday, then hanging out with my mates. My first business was making and selling tarts to delis and gourmet food shops, and although it did well, my career took a different path. I still love making pastry though, and this is the sort of tart I'd serve with a simple salad for brunch or a light lunch. Use freshly grated nutmeg as it gives a far superior flavour to ground.

Serves 6–8

1   To make the shortcrust pastry, place the flour and salt in a bowl and use your fingertips to rub in the butter until the mixture resembles fine crumbs. Make a well in the centre and add the egg and 2 tablespoons chilled water. Mix in gently until a light dough forms. Shape the dough into a disc, wrap in plastic film and put into the fridge for 30 minutes to rest.

2   Preheat the oven to 170°C.

3   Roll out the dough on a clean, lightly floured benchtop until it is 3 mm thick and large enough to cover the base and sides of a round 18 cm tart tin with a removable base. Carefully ease the pastry into the tin and gently press it into the sides, ensuring there are no air pockets. Trim any excess. Use a fork to gently prick the base to prevent the pastry rising.

4   Line the pastry base with baking paper and fill with baking beads or dried rice or beans. Blind bake for 15–20 minutes or until light golden brown, then carefully remove the paper and rice or beans, and bake for a further 5 minutes. Remove from the oven and set aside to cool. Leave the oven on.

5   Cook the speck in a small non-stick frying pan over medium heat until light golden. Transfer to paper towel to drain.

6   Cook the onions in a large saucepan of salted boiling water for 5–6 minutes, until tender. Drain and refresh in iced water. Remove the skins, then halve the onions lengthways. Heat the olive oil in a heavy-based saucepan over low–medium heat, add the onions, cut-side down, and cook for 3–4 minutes or until caramelised. Add the butter and vinegar, stirring to deglaze the pan. Transfer the onions to a bowl and set aside. Blanch the cavolo nero in a saucepan of boiling salted water for 1 minute, then drain and refresh under cold running water.

7   Place the milk in the same saucepan and bring to a simmer over medium heat. Remove from the heat. Stir in the sour cream and egg and season with the cayenne pepper and salt. Pour a little of the egg mixture into the tart shell, then scatter over one-third of the cavolo nero. Repeat in two more batches of egg mixture and cavolo nero. Arrange the speck and onions, caramelised-side up, on top. Bake the tart for 20–30 minutes, until golden brown and cooked through. Serve warm or at room temperature.

4 kg boston butt pork, rind scored, trimmed

brine (see page 208), to cover

1 tablespoon olive oil

4 salad onions, stems trimmed and quartered lengthways

pickling liquid (see page 208), to cover

Spiced pear puree

4 green pears (such as packham)

30 g butter

½ vanilla pod

1 cinnamon stick

1 star anise

2 cloves

2½ tablespoons apple cider vinegar

Pan-roasted pears

40 g butter

2 green pears (such as packham), cored and cut into wedges

Roasted pork with spiced pear puree, pan-roasted pears and pickled onion

Pork and pear is an excellent combination, much in the same way it goes so well with apple. Try to find rare-breed pork as it's fattier and therefore tastier! The 'boston butt' is a square piece of the meat from the shoulder that still has the shoulder blade running through it. It cooks really evenly because of its neat shape and you get the sweeter meat that's close to the bone. Ask your butcher to score the rind for you.

Serves 8–10

1   Place the pork in a container, pour over enough brine to cover, then cover and put into the fridge for 2 hours. Remove the pork and pat dry with paper towel.

2   Preheat the oven to 220°C. Place the pork on a wire rack in a roasting pan and rub over the olive oil. Roast for 20–25 minutes, then reduce the oven temperature to 160°C and roast for a further 2 hours or until cooked through.

3   Meanwhile, to make the spiced pear puree, peel the pears, then quarter, remove the cores and thinly slice. Melt the butter in a heavy-based saucepan over medium heat, add the pear and spices and cook gently for 4 minutes. Add the vinegar and cook for a further 10–15 minutes, until the pear is soft. Add a little water if the pan gets dry during cooking. Remove the spices and discard, then transfer the pear mixture to a food processor or blender and blend until smooth.

4   Place the onion in a heatproof bowl and pour over enough hot pickling liquid to cover. Cover with plastic film and set aside until the onion and liquid have cooled.

5   To make the pan-roasted pears, melt the butter in a heavy-based frying pan over medium heat. Add the pear, cut-side down, and cook for 2 minutes, until golden brown. Turn and cook for 2 minutes, until golden brown. Take off the heat.

6   Slice the roasted pork and serve with the pan-roasted pears, drained pickled onion and spiced pear puree alongside.

2 whole snapper (800 g each), scaled and gutted

1 lemon, sliced

10 g ginger, sliced

salt and pepper

2 spring onions, trimmed and thinly sliced on the diagonal

4 baby bok choy, trimmed and halved lengthways

½ bunch coriander, leaves picked

Ginger and mushroom broth

2 cinnamon sticks

2 star anise

½ cup (125 ml) soy sauce

½ cup (125 ml) mirin

½ cup (125 ml) rice vinegar

2 tablespoons caster sugar

40 g ginger, roughly chopped

2 teaspoons sesame oil

1 punnet (250 g) king brown mushrooms, trimmed and sliced

1 punnet (100 g) enoki mushrooms, trimmed

Steamed snapper with ginger and mushroom broth

Steaming whole fish is a bit of a challenge, but there's nothing better than the sheer delight when you start to serve and see that it's perfectly cooked. You can test it by pressing down with your thumb on the very top of the backbone, near the head. If the flesh starts to give, it is cooked. If king brown mushrooms aren't available, use shimeji or swiss browns instead. Make sure you toast the spices until aromatic, as this releases their natural oils and aromas.

Serves 4

1   To make the ginger and mushroom broth, toast the cinnamon and star anise in a small dry frying pan over medium heat for 1–2 minutes, until lightly toasted and aromatic. Place in a small saucepan with the soy sauce, mirin, rice vinegar, sugar, ginger and 1 cup (250 ml) water and bring to the boil over high heat. Remove from the heat and leave to infuse for 20 minutes, then strain through a fine-meshed sieve and add the sesame oil. Set aside. Add the mushrooms and reheat gently before serving.

2   Use a sharp pair of scissors to cut the fins off the fish and trim the tails. Use a sharp knife to score the flesh three times on each side of the fish. Divide the lemon and ginger slices between the fish cavities. Season the fish with salt and pepper and place on a piece of baking paper.

3   Scatter the spring onion over the top of the fish and place in a double steamer with the bok choy. Steam over high heat for 10–12 minutes, until the fish is cooked through. Place the fish on a serving plate with the bok choy. Finish by spooning over the hot broth and scattering with coriander leaves. Serve.

1 medium potato, peeled and diced

400 g diced blue-eye trevalla fillet

4 raw medium-sized prawns, peeled and deveined

12 clams

1 golden shallot, roughly chopped

1 clove garlic, roughly chopped

100 ml white wine

1 sprig thyme

¼ bunch cavolo nero (Tuscan kale), trimmed

½ cob sweetcorn, kernels removed

140 g cherry tomatoes, quartered

¼ bunch tarragon, leaves picked

toasted sourdough bread, to serve

Sweetcorn veloute

50 g butter

½ brown onion, thinly sliced

1 potato, peeled and thinly sliced

½ stalk lemongrass, roughly chopped and crushed

1 litre chicken stock (see page 206)

5 cobs sweetcorn, kernels removed

salt and pepper

Clam and sweetcorn chowder

I've been a big fan of sweetcorn soup for a long time, going back to when my parents would take us kids to the local Chinese restaurant. Adding seafood to it to make more of a chowder just takes it another step further. Use a mixture of clams – a larger variety, such as diamond, and a smaller one like tua tua, if you can. Baking the chowder instead of cooking it on the stovetop preserves the integrity and texture of the fish as there's no need to stir.

Serves 4

1 To make the sweetcorn veloute, melt the butter in a heavy-based saucepan over medium heat. Add the onion, potato and lemongrass and cook for 5 minutes, until the onion is softened. Add the stock and bring to the boil, skimming off any impurities. Add the corn kernels and cook for a further 2–3 minutes. Remove from the heat and leave to cool slightly. Transfer to a food processor or blender and blend until smooth, then strain through a fine-meshed sieve into a bowl and season with salt and pepper, to taste. Set aside.

2 Preheat the oven to 180°C.

3 Place the potato in a large ovenproof saucepan, cover with cold water and add a pinch of salt. Bring the water to the boil over high heat and cook for 2–3 minutes, until the potato is tender. Drain well.

4 Return the potato to the pan and add the fish, prawns and sweetcorn veloute. Cover and bake for 15 minutes or until the fish is cooked through.

5 Meanwhile, heat a heavy-based saucepan over high heat. Once it is hot, quickly add the clams, shallot, garlic, wine and thyme, then cover tightly and steam for 3–4 minutes, until the clams have opened. Drain the clams, reserving the cooking liquid. Spread the clams over the chowder and pour over the reserved liquid.

6 Cook the cavolo nero and corn kernels in a saucepan of boiling salted water for 30 seconds to 1 minute, then drain well. Arrange on the top of the chowder with the tomato and tarragon. Serve the chowder with toasted sourdough.

100 ml vegetable oil

2 onions, finely diced

2 cloves garlic, finely chopped

30 g ginger, peeled and finely chopped

1 red chilli, seeded and finely chopped

1 tablespoon sweet paprika

5 teaspoons ground cumin

1 teaspoon ground turmeric

1 curry leaf

600 g tomato sauce (see page 209)

1 litre pouring cream

300 ml coconut cream

2 kg chicken thigh fillets, trimmed and cut into 4 cm pieces

250 g unsalted butter, diced

coriander leaves, to garnish

Pilaf

50 g butter

1 onion, finely diced

400 g long-grain white rice

400 ml chicken stock (see page 206)

Butter chicken

I have been making this curry for my friends on the night of the Academy Awards for fifteen years now – they request it every year! Yes, it does use a lot of cream and has a full stick of butter too, but they are essential for a true 'butter chicken' flavour – and I promise you, it's incredibly good.

Serves 8–10

1   Heat the vegetable oil in a large heavy-based saucepan over medium heat and cook the onion, garlic, ginger and chilli for 5 minutes, until the onion is softened. Add the spices and cook for 2–3 minutes, until aromatic, then add the curry leaf and cook for 2 minutes more.

2   Add the tomato sauce and cook for 10 minutes, stirring occasionally to ensure it doesn't stick to the pan. Add the cream and cook for a further 10 minutes, until slightly reduced. Add the coconut cream, chicken and butter and cook for 10–15 minutes or until the chicken is cooked through and the sauce is reduced.

3   Meanwhile, to make the pilaf, melt the butter in a heavy-based saucepan over medium heat. Add the onion and cook for 5 minutes, until softened. Add the rice and stir to coat in the butter and onion. Add the stock and cover with a tight-fitting lid. Increase the heat to medium–high and cook for 9 minutes, then reduce the heat to low and cook for a further 9 minutes or until the rice has absorbed all the stock and is tender.

4   Serve the butter chicken with the pilaf, garnished with coriander leaves.

½ bunch sage, leaves picked

½ bunch rosemary, leaves picked

½ bunch thyme, leaves picked

5 cloves garlic, peeled

300 ml olive oil

200 g ground almonds

40 g salt flakes

1 lamb leg (about 2.5 kg)

1 lemon, zest removed in wide strips

1 litre chicken stock (see page 206)

Roasted lamb with herb and almond crust

This rustic dish may not be the prettiest in the book, but its flavour more than compensates for that. The almonds make a great crust, keeping it all bound together. I suggest serving it with the baby gem, pomegranate and hazelnut salad on page 127.

Serves 6–8

1   Preheat the oven to 150°C.

2   Place the herbs, 2 cloves of garlic and the olive oil in a food processor or blender and process until finely chopped. Add the ground almonds and salt and process until all the ingredients are combined to form a smooth paste.

3   Place the lamb in a deep roasting pan and use a small sharp knife to make 6 incisions, 2 cm wide by 2 cm deep, into the skin. Cut the remaining garlic cloves in half and place in each incision with a piece of lemon zest. Pour the herb paste evenly over the lamb skin, then pour the stock around the lamb. Cover with foil and roast for 3 hours, until the meat comes away from the bone. Remove the foil for the last 5 minutes of cooking. Rest the lamb, covered loosely with foil, for 30 minutes before carving.

^ Baby gem, pomegranate and hazelnut salad

100 g skinned hazelnuts

2 heads baby gem (baby cos) lettuce, leaves separated

1 pomegranate, halved

salt

Hazelnut dressing

35 ml chardonnay vinegar

1 tablespoon honey

½ teaspoon Dijon mustard

150 ml hazelnut oil

25 ml extra virgin olive oil

Baby gem, pomegranate and hazelnut salad

When I was growing up, we always had iceberg lettuce in the fridge. Now, there are loads of varieties, but I still go back to the crisp green lettuces, like iceberg and baby gem. Pomegranate is a favourite new ingredient for me, I love the intense flavour when you bite into the seeds. You could add white anchovies or tinned tuna to make this more substantial.

Serves 4

1 Preheat the oven to 180°C.

2 To make the hazelnut dressing, whisk the vinegar, honey and mustard in a bowl until combined. Slowly add the oils, whisking constantly until emulsified.

3 Spread the hazelnuts over a baking tray and bake for 5–8 minutes or until golden brown. Use a large sharp knife to roughly chop the nuts.

4 Place the lettuce leaves in a bowl and toss through enough dressing to lightly coat (keep the remaining dressing in a jar in the fridge for your next salad). Place on a serving plate and scatter over the hazelnuts. Use the tip of a knife to remove the pomegranate seeds and scatter over the salad. Season with salt and serve.

---

2 bulbs baby fennel, trimmed

½ head cavolo nero (Tuscan kale), trimmed

handful cavolo nero flowers

1 red chilli, seeded and finely chopped

½ bunch dill, leaves picked

⅓ cup (80 ml) classic dressing (see page 210)

salt and pepper

Fennel, cavolo nero, chilli and dill salad

As you're not cooking the cavolo nero, look for a bunch with small leaves, as they'll be more tender with a spicy flavour. If you grow your own cavolo nero and it is in bloom, the little yellow flowers and buds are a lovely addition to this salad.

Serves 4

1 Use a mandoline to thinly slice the fennel and place in a bowl.

2 Add the cavolo nero, flowers, chilli and dill and mix until well combined. Toss through the dressing to lightly coat and season with salt and pepper, to taste. Serve.

^ Fennel, cavolo nero, chilli and dill salad

500 g mixed heirloom tomatoes

40 g Sicilian green olive cheeks

¼ bunch basil, leaves picked

¼ bunch oregano, leaves picked

Olive dressing

30 g Sicilian olive cheeks

finely grated zest of ¼ lemon

25 ml fresh lemon juice

pinch of ground black pepper

½ cup (125 ml) olive oil

Oregano tuile

50 g (⅓ cup) plain flour

1 egg white

45 g butter, melted and cooled

2 teaspoons sugar

15 g confit garlic (see page 194), mashed

¼ teaspoon chopped oregano leaves

small pinch of salt

Salad of tomatoes, crushed green olives and oregano tuile

This is a simple tomato and olive salad that's lifted by a lemony olive dressing and savoury herb tuile. The tuile is a great component – it makes a nice change from croutons and delivers crunch and flavour. Sicilian olives are ideal here, but you could use regular green olives or even kalamata if you like.

Serves 4

1   Preheat the oven to 140°C.

2   To make the oregano tuile, place all the ingredients in a large bowl and whisk until well combined. Spread the mixture evenly over a baking tray lined with baking paper; it should be about 5 mm thick. Bake for 15 minutes or until crisp and just starting to colour.

3   To make the olive dressing, put the olive cheeks, lemon zest, juice and pepper in a mortar and pound with the pestle until the olives are crushed. Stir in the olive oil – the dressing should be chunky, not too smooth.

4   Cut the tomatoes in half or quarters if large. Place in a bowl with the olives, basil and oregano and dress with enough olive dressing to coat (keep any remaining dressing in a jar in the fridge for your next salad). Transfer to a serving bowl, break up the tuile and serve on top of the salad.

2 pieces preserved lemon (see page 194), rind only

8 tomatoes, cut into wedges

¼ bunch oregano, leaves torn

¼ bunch flat-leaf parsley, leaves torn

¼ bunch basil, leaves picked

¼ bunch purple basil, leaves picked

2½ tablespoons extra virgin olive oil

salt and pepper

2 tablespoons balsamic vinegar (preferably 25-year-old)

100 g stracciatella cheese, torn

Tomato, stracciatella, basil and preserved lemon salad

I love experimenting with different varieties of tomatoes. Here, we used the 'Black Russian' variety, which has a rich, sweet tomato flavour and interesting deep-red and green colouring (they almost look black at times, hence the name). Stracciatella is a fresh cheese made from stretched mozzarella and cream that is available from delicatessens and specialty food stores. If unavailable, you can substitute burrata or buffalo mozzarella. You need to use a good-quality balsamic in this recipe – when they're well aged (such as the 25-year-old balsamic) the flavour becomes more balanced and the vinegar thickens naturally.

Serves 4

1   Rinse the preserved lemon rind, cut into matchsticks and place in a bowl with the tomato and herbs. Toss the salad with the olive oil and season with salt and pepper, to taste. Arrange the salad on a serving plate, drizzle with the balsamic vinegar and scatter over the stracciatella. Serve.

salt

250 g quinoa

⅓ cup (80 ml) olive oil

1 red onion, thinly sliced

2 pinches of table salt

⅓ cup (80 ml) chardonnay vinegar

1 telegraph (long) cucumber

1 punnet (250 g) cherry tomatoes, quartered

¼ bunch mint, leaves torn

finely grated zest and juice of 1 lemon

1 clove garlic, finely chopped

150 g marinated feta

Quinoa, cucumber, cherry tomato and feta salad

I really like the versatility of quinoa and have been pairing it with all sorts of different flavours. My wife, Sarah, actually came up with this recipe and I stole it – please don't tell her! I think of it as 'garden salad' quinoa and it's on high rotation at our house.

Serves 4

1   Add enough water to a heavy-based saucepan to come three-quarters of the way up the side, season with salt and bring to the boil over high heat. Add the quinoa and cook for 15 minutes, until it opens up, then drain well. Spread the quinoa over a tray and mix through 1 tablespoon of the olive oil. Cover with plastic film and cool in the fridge.

2   Place the onion in a glass or ceramic bowl with the salt and half the vinegar and leave for 15 minutes to macerate.

3   Cut the cucumber in half lengthways, then use a teaspoon to scoop out the seeds and discard. Slice the cucumber and place in a bowl with the tomato. Drain the onion and add to the salad with the quinoa and mint.

4   Whisk together the lemon zest and juice, garlic and remaining vinegar and olive oil in a small bowl. Toss the dressing through the salad and season with salt and pepper, to taste. Place in a serving bowl, crumble over the feta and serve.

^ Cabbage, radish and herb salad

100 g parmesan

1 bunch cherry belle radishes, trimmed and quartered

¼ white cabbage, shredded

¼ bunch flat-leaf parsley, leaves picked

¼ cup (60 ml) extra virgin olive oil

juice of 2 lemons, or to taste

salt and pepper

1 bunch French breakfast radishes, trimmed

Cabbage, radish and herb salad

Coleslaw is something I like to reinvent every year or so, and this is my latest version, with radishes of course! It works best with two different varieties of red radish, but if you can only get your hands on one, simply use two bunches of it.

Serves 4

1 Finely shred half the parmesan and coarsely grate the rest. Place the shredded parmesan, quartered radishes, cabbage and parsley leaves in a bowl.

2 Lightly dress the salad with the olive oil and lemon juice, to taste, and season with salt and pepper.

3 Use a mandoline to thinly slice the French breakfast radishes and add to the salad with the grated parmesan.

100 g wild rocket, washed and dried

160 g red grapes, halved

100 ml olive oil

juice of 2 lemons, or to taste

60 g parmesan, coarsely grated

Rocket with parmesan and grapes

This salad is best when new-season grapes are available, preferably the red ones rather than the green. Toss them with peppery rocket and a good-quality parmesan – I like reggiano, which has a bit of age – and you have a really simple salad with plenty of interest and a great range of flavours.

Serves 4

1 Put the rocket and grapes into a bowl. Whisk together the olive oil and lemon juice, to taste, until well combined. Season the salad with salt and pepper and toss through enough dressing to lightly coat (keep any remaining dressing in a jar in the fridge for your next salad). Finish with the parmesan and serve.

^ Rocket with parmesan and grapes

100 g baby green beans, topped

ice cubes

1 baby iceberg lettuce

¼ bunch chives, cut into 4 cm lengths

Tarragon dressing

¼ bunch flat-leaf parsley, leaves picked

1 clove garlic, finely chopped

200 ml grapeseed oil

½ bunch tarragon, leaves picked

2 tablespoons chardonnay vinegar

salt and pepper

Iceberg lettuce, chives and baby beans with tarragon dressing

Iceberg lettuce has been a bit eclipsed by all the newer varieties, so it's easy to forget how good it really is, but there is a reason why it's stood the test of time, and that's crunch. Here, it is dressed up with green beans split lengthways, which is such a neat trick – just break them at the top and then split them using your hands.

Serves 4

1   Cook the beans in a saucepan of salted boiling water for 2–3 minutes, until bright green and tender crisp. Drain and refresh in iced water. When the beans have cooled, split them in half lengthways.

2   To make the tarragon dressing, place the parsley and garlic in a blender with half the grapeseed oil and blend until smooth. Add the tarragon and blend, slowly adding the rest of the oil with the motor running. Transfer to a mixing bowl and stir through the vinegar. Season with salt and pepper, to taste.

3   Cut the lettuce into wedges, separate the leaves a bit and place on a plate with the split beans. Scatter over the chives and enough tarragon dressing to lightly coat (keep the remaining dressing in a jar in the fridge for your next salad). Serve.

4 green zucchini (courgettes), trimmed

¼ bunch mint, finely chopped

¼ bunch flat-leaf parsley, finely chopped

½ clove garlic, finely chopped

finely grated zest and juice of 1 lemon

100 ml olive oil

salt and pepper

½ cup (75 g) skinned hazelnuts, roasted and roughly chopped

dill sprigs, to serve

Raw zucchini, hazelnuts, lemon and herbs

This dish was created by a friend of mine who has a blog called Lucy in the Larder. Lucy's a great home cook and she made this for British food and cookery writer Hugh Fearnley Whittingstall and he raved about it to me. Zucchini is generally cooked, but this is a very simple and delicious way to use it. If you can get yellow or baby zucchini, a mixture would work really well. You could substitute pattypan squash, if you like.

Serves 4

1   Use a mandoline to slice the zucchini into long ribbons and place in a bowl with the mint and parsley.

2   Whisk together the garlic and lemon zest and juice, then slowly whisk in the olive oil until well combined.

3   Toss enough of the dressing through the zucchini salad to lightly coat (keep any remaining dressing in a jar in the fridge for your next salad) and season with salt and pepper. Place on a serving plate and sprinkle over the hazelnuts and dill.

^ Green beans, confit shallot and fried capers

5 golden shallots, finely diced

2 cups (500 ml) vegetable oil

2 teaspoons pickled capers, rinsed

480 g green beans, topped

Green beans, confit shallot and fried capers

Capers are a flower bud and when you fry them they burst open, so it's like eating little crispy flowers. When paired with the sweetness and crunch of confit shallots, they take these beans to another level.

Serves 4

1   Place the shallot in a small heavy-based saucepan with half the vegetable oil and bring to a simmer over low heat. Simmer gently until translucent and tender. Remove from the heat, drain off half the oil and discard, then set the confit shallot aside.

2   Heat the remaining oil in a heavy-based saucepan over high heat to 180°C (a cube of bread will brown in 20 seconds). Fry the capers for 2–3 minutes, until crisp, then transfer to paper towel to drain.

3   Cook the beans in a large saucepan of boiling salted water for 3–4 minutes or until bright green and tender crisp. Drain well and place in a bowl. Toss through the confit shallot, then transfer to a plate and finish with the fried capers.

---

2 heads broccoli, cut into florets

1½ tablespoons extra virgin olive oil

1 golden shallot, finely diced

1 long red chilli, finely chopped

1 clove garlic, finely chopped

salt

Broccoli with chilli and garlic

This is the sort of thing I do at home all the time. You could use just about any vegetable instead of broccoli here – broccolini, cauliflower, Brussels sprouts, the list goes on. It's a really low-fuss, tasty way to serve vegies.

Serves 4

1   Cook the broccoli in a large saucepan of boiling salted water for 3–4 minutes or until tender. Drain well.

2   Meanwhile, heat the olive oil in a large heavy-based frying pan over high heat. Add the shallot, chilli and garlic and cook, stirring, for 2 minutes. Add the broccoli and gently toss to coat in the chilli mixture. Season with salt and serve.

Broccoli with chilli and garlic

3 cups (750 ml) milk

125 g instant polenta

75 g unsalted butter

75 g parmesan, finely grated

salt and pepper

100 g crème fraîche

30 g salted butter

150 g swiss brown mushrooms, thickly sliced

150 g chestnut mushrooms, trimmed

¼ bunch flat-leaf parsley, finely chopped

parmesan shavings, to serve

2 teaspoons truffle oil, to drizzle

Soft polenta with mixed mushrooms and parmesan

You can use whatever mushrooms are available in this dish, but do try to get at least two different types. I like to use pine mushrooms when they're in season. Four generations of my family have lived in the Oberon region of NSW and my family farm, Green Hills, is also in that area. It's well known for its vast pine forests and in summer and autumn you can find masses of pine mushrooms. I often go foraging up there with a couple of chefs. This is a lovely side dish for chicken and lamb.

Serves 4

1 Bring the milk to the boil in a heavy-based saucepan over medium heat. Add the polenta in a slow steady stream and whisk until thickened, about 3–4 minutes. Reduce the heat to low, add the unsalted butter and whisk until combined, then add the parmesan and whisk until the cheese is melted and combined. Season with salt and pepper, to taste, and fold through the crème fraîche.

2 Melt the salted butter in a heavy-based frying pan over high heat. When it starts to foam add the mushrooms and saute for 2–4 minutes, until tender. Season with salt and pepper, to taste, and mix through the parsley.

3 Spoon the polenta onto a shallow bowl, top with the sauteed mushrooms and parmesan shavings, and drizzle over the truffle oil. Serve.

1 spaghetti squash

1 dumpling pumpkin

½ teaspoon Chinese five-spice powder

2 cloves garlic, halved

20 g butter, chopped

salt and pepper

2½ tablespoons olive oil

1½ tablespoons chardonnay vinegar

2 tablespoons honey

salt and pepper

1 pickled jalapeño (see page 200), sliced

micro-coriander, to garnish

Lime-roasted almonds

1 egg white

finely grated zest and juice of 1 lime

½ cup (80 g) blanched almonds

Lime yoghurt

80 g Greek-style yoghurt

finely grated zest and juice of 1 lime

salt

Baked spiced pumpkin with lime-roasted almonds and pickled jalapeño

Spaghetti squash is a really unusual vegetable. It's from the squash family and looks a bit like a small pale-yellow watermelon. When it's cooked the flesh inside comes apart in strands, like spaghetti. It's a great alternative to pasta. If you can't find it, make double the baked dumpling pumpkin instead. Chinese five-spice sets off the pumpkin perfectly, and the lime-roasted almonds add a contrasting crunch. I usually make extra almonds to keep for a snack.

Serves 4

1 To make the lime-roasted almonds, preheat the oven to 180°C. Use an electric mixer to whisk the egg white in a small bowl to soft peaks, then whisk in the lime zest and juice. Using a slotted spoon, coat the almonds in the egg white mixture, then drain off any excess and scatter over a baking tray lined with baking paper. Bake for 6 minutes, until the nuts are golden. Remove from the oven and set aside to cool, then cut the almonds in half.

2 To make the lime yoghurt, whisk together the yoghurt, lime zest and juice in a bowl. Season with salt, to taste, then cover with plastic film and put into the fridge until needed.

3 Bring a large heavy-based saucepan of water to the boil over high heat. Add the whole spaghetti squash and boil for 45 minutes. Drain and leave to cool.

4 Meanwhile, cut the dumpling pumpkin in half and scoop out the seeds. Sprinkle the inside of the pumpkin with the five-spice, dot the garlic and butter over the spice and season well with salt and pepper. Put the pumpkin halves back together, wrap in foil and bake for 30–40 minutes, until the pumpkin is soft. Take out of the oven, remove the foil and cut into small wedges, leaving the skin intact.

5 Cut the cooled spaghetti squash in half and remove the seeds. Use your hands to break the flesh down into spaghetti-like strands – it should come away from the skin easily. Place 300 g of the strands in a heavy-based saucepan with the olive oil, vinegar and honey and stir over medium heat until hot. (Keep any remaining strands for another use.) Season with salt and pepper, to taste.

6 Arrange the spaghetti squash and pumpkin wedges on a plate. Scatter over the lime-roasted almonds and jalapeño, and drizzle with the lime yoghurt. Garnish with micro-coriander and serve.

600 g small kipfler potatoes, scrubbed

2½ tablespoons olive oil

4 cloves garlic, unpeeled and halved

¼ bunch thyme

2 sprigs rosemary, leaves picked

salt and pepper

¼ cup (60 ml) white vinegar

ice cubes

5 quail eggs, at room temperature

100 g fresh shelled peas (from about 200 g peas in pods)

80 g salted capers, rinsed and dried

½ bunch chives, cut into 5 cm lengths

100 ml classic dressing (see page 210)

Crushed potatoes with peas, capers and quail eggs

When I was growing up, potato salad was a pretty regular fixture at mealtimes, particularly around Christmas. Waxy varieties, like kipfler, weren't available back then, but they're the best bet for a salad. While my mother's version was pretty good, I've made a few changes: soft-boiled quail eggs whose runny yolks contribute to the dressing and the addition of peas for colour and texture – and to compensate for flicking them onto the floor as a kid!

Serves 4

1 Preheat the oven to 180°C.

2 Place the potatoes on a baking tray and toss with the olive oil, garlic, thyme and rosemary. Season with salt and pepper and bake for 30–40 minutes, until tender when tested with a skewer. Take out of the oven and use the back of a fork to roughly crush the potatoes.

3 Meanwhile, add the vinegar to a bowl of iced water. Bring a small saucepan of water to a rapid boil over high heat. Gently add the quail eggs to the pan and cook for 1 minute 30 seconds, then transfer to the vinegar water and leave for 15 minutes (the vinegar will soften the shells, making the eggs easier to peel).

4 Bring a small saucepan of salted water to the boil over high heat. Cook the peas for 3 minutes, until tender. Drain and refresh in iced water, then roughly chop, leaving some whole.

5 Place the capers in a serving bowl with the peas and potato. Gently toss through the chives and dressing, and season with salt and pepper.

6 Carefully peel the quail eggs, then cut in half and dot over the salad.

1 red capsicum (pepper)

1 green capsicum (pepper)

2 bulbs baby fennel, 4 fronds reserved

1 zucchini (courgette)

1 red onion, cut into 6–8 wedges

salt and pepper

2½ tablespoons olive oil

1½ tablespoons cabernet sauvignon vinegar

finely grated zest of ½ lemon

1 clove garlic, finely chopped

1 sprig thyme

1 sprig rosemary

1 punnet (250 g) cherry tomatoes, bases scored

⅓ cup (80 ml) ginger and shallot sauce (see page 210)

½ bunch flat-leaf parsley, leaves picked

½ bunch basil, leaves picked

½ bunch mint, leaves picked

Oven-baked vegetables

This dish is inspired by my loyal 'brother from another mother', Simon Sandall, who has worked with me for fifteen years. He came in one day and showed me a picture of it and I borrowed the recipe for this book. It's clean and fresh, the way all good food should be. You can substitute any vegetables that are in season.

Serves 4

1 Preheat the oven to 180°C.

2 Halve the capsicums and remove the seeds, then cut into randomly sized pieces and place in a large roasting pan. Cut the fennel and zucchini into randomly sized pieces and add to the pan with the onion. Season the vegetables with salt and pepper and toss together with the olive oil, vinegar, lemon zest, garlic, thyme and rosemary. Bake for 20–25 minutes, until golden and tender, adding the tomatoes for the last 5 minutes of cooking. Remove from the oven, toss through the ginger and shallot sauce and season with salt and pepper, to taste.

3 Just before serving, scatter with the reserved fennel fronds and the herbs.

1 large cauliflower

⅔ cup (160 ml) rosemary-infused olive oil

3 sprigs thyme

juice of 1 lemon

small handful picked watercress leaves

¼ bunch oregano, leaves picked

1 tablespoon pickled capers, to serve

Caper and raisin dressing

2 teaspoons raisins

2 tablespoons verjuice

2 tablespoons pickled capers, rinsed

Roasted cauliflower with caper and raisin dressing

There's a bit of a stigma around cauliflower. People think it has a strong flavour and they won't like it, but it's actually pretty mild and one of the most versatile vegies around. It can be steamed, mashed, roasted, pureed or baked. Here, it's pan-fried and then finished in the oven and served with sweet raisins and salty capers.

Serves 4

1 Preheat the oven to 180°C.

2 To make the caper and raisin dressing, place the raisins and verjuice in a small heavy-based saucepan and bring to the boil over medium heat. Stir in the capers, then spoon the mixture into a small food processor or the chopper bowl of a stick mixer. Process to a smooth puree, then press through a fine-meshed sieve. If you have trouble blending the ingredients, add a little more verjuice.

3 Break the cauliflower down into 8 large florets, then cut each in half lengthways through the core to make 16 pieces.

4 Heat 150 ml of the rosemary oil and the thyme sprigs in a large ovenproof frying pan over high heat. Add the cauliflower and cook for 2 minutes each side, until golden. Place the pan in the oven for 3–4 minutes, until the cauliflower is tender.

5 Sprinkle the lemon juice and remaining rosemary oil over the cauliflower. Transfer to a plate and drizzle with the dressing. Scatter over the watercress, oregano and capers and serve.

4 bulbs fennel, trimmed and tough outer layers removed

⅓ cup (80 ml) vegetable oil

3 cloves garlic

4 sprigs thyme

1 sprig rosemary

300 ml chicken stock (see page 206)

200 ml pouring cream

60 g blue cheese, crumbled

2 cups (100 g) panko breadcrumbs

dill sprigs, to garnish

Ask the butcher's wife

I love this dish of baked fennel with blue cheese and crisp panko breadcrumbs. I tried it when I was visiting my best mate Anthony Puharich, from Vic's Meat and the *Ask the Butcher* TV show. His wife, Rebecca, made it for us and it was unbelievable.

Serves 4

1   Preheat the oven to 180°C.

2   Cut each fennel bulb into quarters.

3   Heat the oil in a heavy-based frying pan over medium heat. Add the fennel, garlic cloves and herbs and cook for 2–3 minutes, until the fennel is golden underneath. Turn the fennel and cook until golden on the other side. Add the chicken stock and cook, turning the fennel often, until it has reduced to a glaze.

4   Transfer the fennel to a casserole dish and strain over the reduced stock, discarding the garlic and herbs. Pour in the cream, mix through the blue cheese and sprinkle over the breadcrumbs. Bake for 8–10 minutes, until the breadcrumbs are golden. Garnish with the dill and serve hot.

2 eggs

2 cups (320 g) fresh shelled peas
(from about 600 g peas in pods)

ice cubes

100 g sourdough bread

200 ml vegetable oil

1½ tablespoons olive oil

1 golden shallot, thinly sliced

80 g bacon, cut into thin strips

¼ bunch mint, leaves shredded

1 piece preserved lemon
(see page 194), rind only

salt and pepper

60 g soft goat's cheese (chevre)

small handful pea shoots, to garnish

62-degree egg with goat's cheese, bacon, peas and preserved lemon

You're probably wondering whether the slow, controlled cooking required here is really worthwhile. All I can say is please try it once. Yes, it's time consuming, but it gives these eggs an amazing texture – more gooey, thicker and softer than a regular boiled egg. The consistency pulls all the other ingredients together, but you could use soft-boiled eggs instead if you're pressed for time. Serve this dish on two plates, with one egg for each portion.

Serves 4

1 Fill a small heavy-based saucepan with the hottest water from the tap and carefully add the eggs. Place on the lowest heat possible and bring to 62°C. Check the water's temperature with a thermometer every few minutes to ensure it stays at 62°C. If the temperature gets too high, add a little cold water to bring it back down. Cook the eggs at 62°C for 45 minutes, then take off the heat and let the eggs sit in the water for 15 minutes.

2 Meanwhile, place the shelled peas in a saucepan of salted boiling water and blanch for 1–2 minutes, until tender. Drain and refresh in a bowl of iced water.

3 Remove the crust from the sourdough bread and discard, then tear the bread into bite-sized pieces. Heat the vegetable oil in a heavy-based saucepan over high heat to 180°C (a cube of bread will brown in 20 seconds). Add the bread and cook until lightly browned, then transfer to paper towel to drain.

4 Heat the olive oil in a non-stick frying pan over medium heat and cook the shallot until softened. Add the bacon and cook until light golden. Drain the peas, add to the pan and cook, tossing, until warmed. Toss through the mint and remove from the heat.

5 Rinse the preserved lemon rind, cut into thin strips and toss through the pea mixture. Season with salt and pepper, to taste. Transfer to 2 serving dishes and scatter over the croutons and goat's cheese. Gently crack an egg into the middle of each, garnish with the pea shoots and serve.

1 punnet (150 g) raspberries, halved

1 punnet (125 g) blueberries

1 punnet (250 g) strawberries, hulled and quartered

edible flowers and leaves, to garnish

Raspberry sorbet

½ leaf gold-strength gelatine

3 teaspoons fresh lemon juice

1½ tablespoons liquid glucose

35 g caster sugar

250 g raspberries

Meringues

4 egg whites, at room temperature

1 cup (220 g) caster sugar

200 g icing sugar mixture

1 teaspoon white vinegar

1 teaspoon cornflour

Passionfruit curd

16 passionfruit

310 g butter

100 g caster sugar

3 eggs

1 leaf gold-strength gelatine

Berries and meringue with passionfruit curd

This one's for the ladies – instead of giving them flowers, you should be making this dish. That said, you may be better reverting to the flower option if the weather is wet or humid, as it will make your meringues weep. All the components could be made individually, too; the meringues served simply with berries and cream, the sorbet served with biscotti and the passionfruit curd served in mini tart cases or with scones.

Serves 4

1. To make the raspberry sorbet, soften the gelatine in cold water for 30 seconds. Remove and squeeze out any excess water. Bring the lemon juice, glucose, sugar, raspberries and 1 cup (250 ml) water to a simmer in a small heavy-based saucepan over medium heat and whisk until the sugar has dissolved. Remove from the heat and whisk in the gelatine, until dissolved. Churn in an ice-cream machine according to the manufacturer's instructions, then freeze until firm.

2. Preheat the oven to 80°C. Line 2 baking trays with baking paper.

3. To make the meringues, use an electric mixer to whisk the egg whites in a clean, dry bowl on high speed until foamy. Gradually add the sugar, a little at a time, whisking constantly until the sugar dissolves and the mixture forms firm peaks. Gradually add the icing sugar the same way. Use a large metal spoon to fold in the vinegar and cornflour until well combined.

4. Place the meringue in a piping bag fitted with a 15 mm fluted nozzle and pipe onto the lined tray. Use a kitchen blowtorch to scorch the top of each meringue. Bake the meringues for 2 hours or until dry on the outside and chewy on the inside. Remove and set aside on the trays to cool.

5. To make the passionfruit curd, cut 15 of the passionfruit in half and scoop out the pulp. Set a fine-meshed sieve over a bowl and press the passionfruit pulp through the sieve. Discard the seeds. Heat the butter and sieved passionfruit pulp in a small saucepan over low heat, stirring often, until melted and combined.

6. Meanwhile, use an electric mixer to whisk the caster sugar and eggs until thick and pale. Take the passionfruit mixture off the heat and whisk in the egg mixture, then return to low heat and stir constantly until the mixture has a custard consistency and coats the back of a spoon. Soften the gelatine in cold water for 30 seconds. Remove and squeeze out any excess water, then whisk through the custard. Press the mixture through a fine-meshed sieve. Scoop out the pulp from the remaining passionfruit, whisk into the curd and place in the fridge to cool.

7. To serve, spread 2 tablespoons of the passionfruit curd over the base of each plate. Arrange the berries in a pile in the centre, place the meringues in and around them and garnish with the flowers, leaves and a scoop of sorbet.

1 punnet (150 g) raspberries, halved

1 punnet (250 g) strawberries, hulled and quartered

1 punnet (125 g) blueberries, halved

Panna cotta

100 g good-quality white chocolate, chopped

300 ml milk

70 g caster sugar

3 leaves gold-strength gelatine

300 ml pouring cream

Strawberry jelly

2 punnets (250 g each) strawberries, hulled and roughly chopped

⅓ cup (75 g) caster sugar

3 leaves gold-strength gelatine

White chocolate panna cotta

This panna cotta makes such a beautiful finish to a meal – it's silky smooth, a little bit rich and a little bit tart. It's glamorous enough to serve at a dinner party, yet simple enough to make for a family meal. You could leave out the jelly if you're short on time.

Serves 4

1 To make the panna cotta, place the chocolate in a heatproof bowl. Bring the milk and sugar to a simmer in a heavy-based saucepan over medium heat, stirring to dissolve the sugar. Soften the gelatine in cold water for 30 seconds, then remove and squeeze out any excess water. Add to the hot milk mixture and stir until dissolved, then pour over the chocolate and whisk until melted and combined. Whisk in the cream, then divide among four serving glasses and place in the fridge for at least 6 hours to set.

2 To make the strawberry jelly, place the strawberries and sugar in a heatproof bowl and wrap the bowl tightly in plastic film. Place over a saucepan of simmering water and cook for 15–20 minutes, until a pool of liquid forms in the bowl. Remove the bowl from the pan and strain the liquid through a fine-meshed sieve. Stir in 100 ml water. Soften the gelatine in cold water for 30 seconds, then squeeze out any excess water. Add to the hot strawberry liquid and stir until dissolved. Set aside for 10 minutes to cool a little.

3 Once the panna cotta has set, pour a thin layer of strawberry jelly over the top of each, then return to the fridge to set.

4 To serve, arrange the berries on top of each panna cotta.

400 g sugar

1 tablespoon green tea leaves

2½ tablespoons fresh lemon juice

4 beurre bosc pears, peeled

edible flowers, to garnish

Toasted rice ice-cream

65 g jasmine rice

1½ cups (375 ml) full-cream milk

4 egg yolks

⅓ cup (75 g) caster sugar

140 ml pouring cream

Puffed rice

50 g jasmine rice

2 cups (500 ml) vegetable oil

Pears poached in green tea with toasted rice ice-cream

One of the first desserts I ever learnt to cook was Pear Hélène, at French restaurant La Belle Helene. I've always loved pears – we had a pear tree on the farm where I grew up – but poaching them was a revelation. Here, they're served with toasted rice ice-cream, which may sound odd but has a beautiful nutty flavour, and puffed rice to give a bit of crunch.

Serves 4

1   To make the toasted rice ice-cream, preheat the oven to 180°C and line a baking tray with baking paper. Spread the rice over the lined tray and bake for 5–8 minutes or until all the grains are golden. Remove from the oven and set aside.

2   Put the milk into a large saucepan over medium heat and bring to a gentle simmer. Add the toasted rice, then take off the heat and set aside for 30 minutes to infuse.

3   Use a balloon whisk to whisk the egg yolks and sugar in a bowl until well combined. Return the infused milk to low heat, add the egg yolk mixture and use a wooden spoon to stir constantly until the custard thickens and coats the back of the spoon; this should take 10–15 minutes. Strain the custard through a fine-meshed sieve (do not push the rice through the sieve); discard the rice. Cover with plastic film and poke a hole in the top, then place in the fridge to cool. Once cooled, add the cream and stir to combine. Churn in an ice-cream machine according to the manufacturer's instructions, then freeze until firm.

4   To make the puffed rice, preheat the oven to 100°C. Cook the rice in a saucepan of boiling water for 8 minutes, then drain well. Spread evenly over a baking tray lined with baking paper and bake for 1–2 hours or until crisp and dry.

5   Heat the oil in a heavy-based saucepan over medium–high heat to 180°C (a cube of bread will brown in 20 seconds). Add the rice quickly and stir to disperse through the oil. Once the rice puffs up, immediately use a slotted spoon to remove it and place on paper towel to drain. You need to work very quickly to avoid the rice burning.

6   Put 1.5 litres water in a large heavy-based saucepan, add the sugar and bring to a simmer over medium heat, stirring to dissolve the sugar. Stir in the tea leaves and lemon juice. Add the pears and simmer over low heat for 15–20 minutes, until tender. Take off the heat and let the pears cool in the liquid.

7   To serve, place the pears in serving bowls with a scoop of the toasted rice ice-cream. Sprinkle with the puffed rice, spoon over some of the poaching liquid and garnish with flowers.

SWEET

1 mango, peeled, stone removed,
flesh cut into cubes

250 g mixed berries

¼ cup (60 ml) fresh orange juice

4 scoops good-quality vanilla ice-cream
(see page 178)

icing sugar, to dust

Strawberry jelly

2 punnets (250 g each) strawberries,
hulled and roughly chopped

80 g caster sugar

2½ tablespoons verjuice

3½ leaves gold-strength gelatine

Meringue

2 egg whites, at room temperature

130 g caster sugar

Sponge

5 eggs

120 g sugar

120 g plain flour

Chantilly cream

1 cup (250 ml) thickened cream

¼ cup (40 g) icing sugar mixture

½ vanilla bean, split lengthways
and seeds scraped

Knickerbocker glory

We had a lot of fun creating
this dessert. It's reminiscent
of an English-style trifle, but
it's much messier, and tastier,
too. You can layer it however
you like and adjust the fruit
according to what's in season.

Serves 4

1 For the strawberry jelly, place the strawberries and sugar in a heatproof bowl and
wrap the bowl tightly in plastic film. Place over a saucepan of simmering water
and cook for 15–20 minutes, until a pool of liquid forms in the bowl. Remove from
the pan and strain the liquid through a fine-meshed sieve. Place the strawberry
liquid, ⅓ cup (80 ml) water and the verjuice in a small heavy-based saucepan
and heat to 80°C on a sugar thermometer. Remove from the heat. Soften the
gelatine in cold water for 30 seconds, then squeeze out any excess water. Add
to the strawberry mixture and whisk until dissolved. Place in a container and
put into the fridge until set.

2 For the meringue, preheat the oven to 120°C. Line a baking tray with baking
paper. Use an electric mixer to whisk the egg whites in a clean, dry bowl on high
speed until foamy. Gradually add the sugar, a little at a time, whisking constantly
until the sugar dissolves and the mixture forms firm peaks. Place the meringue
in a piping bag fitted with a 15 mm nozzle and pipe long straight rows onto the
tray. Bake for 30–45 minutes or until crisp and dry. Set aside on the tray to cool.
Increase the oven temperature to 170°C.

3 To make the sponge, grease a round 18 cm cake tin with melted butter and line
with baking paper. Use an electric mixer to whisk the eggs and sugar on high
speed until pale and fluffy. Transfer to a mixing bowl, gently sift over some of the
flour and lightly fold through. Continue adding the flour this way, folding in a little
at a time to keep the mixture airy, until it is all incorporated. Spoon the mixture
into the prepared tin and bake for 15 minutes or until golden and a skewer
inserted into the centre comes out clean. Allow to stand for 5 minutes before
turning out onto a wire rack to cool.

4 To make the Chantilly cream, use an electric mixer to whisk the cream, icing
sugar and vanilla seeds to soft peaks.

5 Use a spoon to break up the strawberry jelly. Rip the sponge into bite-sized
pieces and break up the meringue. Layer the jelly, mango, mixed berries, sponge,
meringue and Chantilly cream in four glasses, then drizzle with the orange juice
and top with a scoop of vanilla ice-cream. Dust with icing sugar and serve.

1¼ cups (250 g) carnaroli rice

1 cup (250 ml) milk

1 cup (250 ml) coconut cream

120 g caster sugar

1 vanilla bean, split lengthways
and seeds scraped

3 egg yolks

8 strawberries, hulled and diced

edible flowers, to garnish

micro-coriander, to garnish

Strawberry sorbet

½ leaf gold-strength gelatine

3 teaspoons fresh lemon juice

35 g caster sugar

30 g liquid glucose

500 g strained pureed strawberries

Honey crisps

90 g honey

80 g butter

4 thin slices rye bread, halved

Strawberry jam

1 punnet (250 g) strawberries,
hulled and chopped

90 g caster sugar

25 ml fresh lemon juice

Rice-vinegar caramel

65 g caster sugar

35 ml rice vinegar

juice of ½ lemon

Vanilla rice pudding with strawberry sorbet and honey crisps

My oldest memory of any dessert
is rice pudding – my nan used
to make a delicious baked one.
Now, I make rice pudding for my
kids, but I like to add some extra
touches to balance the richness.
In this version, there's cold and
tart sorbet, crunchy honey crisps
and sweet jam. Perfection.

Serves 4

1   To make the strawberry sorbet, soften the gelatine in cold water for 30 seconds.
    Remove and squeeze out any excess water. Bring the lemon juice, sugar and
    glucose to a simmer in a small heavy-based saucepan over medium heat and
    whisk until the sugar has dissolved. Remove from the heat and whisk in the
    gelatine, until dissolved. Add the strawberry puree and 200 ml water and mix
    until combined. Churn in an ice-cream machine according to the manufacturer's
    instructions, then freeze until firm.

2   Preheat the oven to 150°C.

3   To make the honey crisps, line a baking tray with baking paper. Heat the honey
    and butter in a saucepan over medium heat until melted and combined. Dip the
    bread in the honey mix, then place on the lined tray. Bake for 10–20 minutes, until
    the bread is caramelised and crisp. Set aside.

4   Meanwhile, to make the strawberry jam, put the strawberries, sugar and lemon
    juice into a small heavy-based saucepan over medium heat and stir to combine.
    Bring to a simmer, stirring constantly until the strawberries break down and the
    mixture has a jam-like consistency. Take off the heat and set aside to cool.

5   Place the rice, milk, coconut cream, sugar, vanilla seeds and pod, and 1 cup
    (250 ml) water in a rice cooker and cook, stirring occasionally, for 15 minutes
    or until the liquid is absorbed. Remove the bowl from the cooker and stir in
    the egg yolks. Cover to keep warm.

6   For the rice-vinegar caramel, heat the sugar in a small heavy-based saucepan
    over medium heat until it melts to make a light golden caramel. Carefully add
    the vinegar and 25 ml water, stirring to deglaze the pan, and cook until reduced
    to a glaze. Add the lemon juice to finish.

7   To serve, remove the vanilla pod and divide the rice pudding among serving
    bowls. Top with the strawberry jam, honey crisps and diced strawberries and
    serve with a scoop of sorbet and a drizzle of the caramel. Garnish with flowers
    and micro-coriander.

5 green apples, peeled, cored and cut into bite-sized pieces

60 g brown sugar

finely grated zest and juice of ½ lemon

1 tablespoon apple cider vinegar

10 g butter

½ vanilla bean, split lengthways and seeds scraped

1 star anise

pinch of ground cinnamon

whipped cream, ice-cream or custard, to serve

Crumble

⅔ cup (100 g) plain flour

¼ cup (55 g) demerara sugar

50 g butter, chopped and softened

Apple crumble

If I ever needed proof that comfort food will never go out of favour, this apple crumble is it. It's been a massive seller at Chiswick restaurant ever since we put it on the menu. I like to keep the texture of the apple, rather than stewing it too much, so we cook the crumble separately, then combine them right at the end. I like to use granny smith apples in this recipe, as it's a true Australian variety.

Serves 4

1   Preheat the oven to 170°C.

2   Combine the apple, sugar, lemon zest and juice, vinegar, butter, vanilla seeds and pod, star anise and cinnamon in a casserole dish. Bake for 30 minutes or until the apple is just softened. Remove the vanilla pod and star anise.

3   Meanwhile, to make the crumble, combine the flour and sugar in a large bowl and use your fingertips to rub in the butter until the mixture comes together in small clumps. Scatter over a baking tray and bake for 10 minutes or until golden brown.

4   Divide the apple mixture among individual baking dishes or leave in the casserole dish. Scatter the crumble over the top and bake for 5 minutes. Serve with whipped cream, ice-cream or custard.

12 apricots

2 litres sugar syrup (see page 211)

1 vanilla bean

2 sprigs rosemary

2 star anise

Rough puff pastry

200 g butter

1⅓ cups (200 g) plain flour, plus extra for dusting

pinch of salt

splash of white vinegar

2 egg yolks, lightly beaten, for glazing

Vanilla ice-cream

2 cups (500 ml) milk

½ vanilla bean, split lengthways and seeds scraped

12 egg yolks

½ cup (110 g) caster sugar

1 cup (250 ml) pouring cream

Almond cream

50 g butter, softened

50 g ground almonds

⅓ cup (55 g) icing sugar mixture

1 small egg

1 teaspoon cornflour

1 teaspoon dark rum

Apricot caramel glaze

¼ cup (55 g) caster sugar

25 g butter

1 scant tablespoon liquid glucose

35 g apricot puree (bought or homemade)

1 sprig rosemary, leaves picked

Apricot and rosemary tarts

I know this sounds like a strange combination, but trust me, it works. Apricots are only around for a short period of time in summer, so I try to buy them in bulk and preserve them. If you have some preserved apricots on hand, just skip step 6. For the best result, make the pastry the day before so it has 24 hours to rest.

Serves 4

1 To make the rough puff pastry, knead 150 g of the butter and 60 g of the flour together to form a dough. Place in between two sheets of plastic film or baking paper and use a rolling pin to roll into a long, thin rectangular shape, about 30 cm × 15 cm. Place in the fridge for 2 hours to rest.

2 Meanwhile, knead the remaining 50 g butter and 140 g flour together to form a dough. Add the salt, vinegar and ¼ cup (60 ml) water and knead to combine, being careful not to overwork the dough. Shape into a disc, wrap in plastic film and place in the fridge for 2 hours to rest.

3 Remove the doughs from the fridge. Remove the baking paper or plastic film from the rolled dough and place on a floured benchtop. Unwrap the disc of dough, place on the floured benchtop and roll into a long, thin rectangular shape, about the same size as the other piece of dough. Lay on top of the already-rolled dough and make a double fold, by folding each side into the middle and then one side over the other (like you're closing a book). Wrap in plastic film and place in the fridge for a further 2 hours to rest. Repeat the rolling and folding, then wrap up again and rest the pastry for 24 hours in the fridge (this will give the best result, but you could get away with a minimum of 2 hours).

4 Meanwhile, to make the vanilla ice-cream, bring the milk and vanilla seeds and pod to a gentle simmer in a saucepan over medium heat, then take off the heat. Remove the vanilla pod. Use a balloon whisk to whisk the egg yolks and sugar in a mixing bowl until thick and pale, then add to the warm milk and whisk until combined. Cook over low heat, using a wooden spoon to stir constantly, until the custard thickens and coats the back of the spoon. Remove from the heat and transfer to a bowl, then cover with plastic film and set aside to cool. Stir in the cream, then churn in an ice-cream machine according to the manufacturer's instructions and freeze until firm.

❯

SWEET

	Almond ice-cream	Candied oranges
1 orange, well washed	100 g slivered almonds	500 g caster sugar
3 eggs	2 cups (500 ml) milk	½ vanilla bean
1 cup (125 g) ground almonds	12 egg yolks	1 cinnamon stick
125 g caster sugar	½ cup (110 g) caster sugar	1 star anise
¼ teaspoon baking powder	1 cup (250 ml) pouring cream	1 orange, cut into 2 mm-thick slices
1 punnet (150 g) raspberries		
icing sugar, for dusting		

Flourless orange cake with almond ice-cream, raspberries and orange

As with all almond-based cakes, this is wonderfully dense and moist, so you only need small portions. Blood oranges would make it slightly darker in colour, but the flavour would be delicious. You could serve this cake with the poached pears on page 170 when raspberries aren't in season.

Serves 4

1   To make the almond ice-cream, preheat the oven to 180°C. Spread the almonds over a baking tray and roast for 6 minutes, until golden. Remove from the oven.

2   Put the milk and almonds in a saucepan and bring to a gentle simmer over medium heat. Take off the heat and set aside for 15 minutes to infuse. Strain through a fine-meshed sieve and return the milk to the pan; discard the almonds. Use a balloon whisk to whisk the egg yolks and sugar in a bowl until combined, then add to the milk and whisk to combine. Cook over low–medium heat, using a wooden spoon to stir constantly, until the custard thickens and coats the back of the spoon. Remove from the heat and transfer to a container, then cover and set aside to cool. Add the cream and stir to combine. Churn in an ice-cream machine according to the manufacturer's instructions, then freeze until firm.

3   To make the candied oranges, place the sugar, vanilla bean, cinnamon, star anise and 2 cups (500 ml) water in a heavy-based saucepan and bring to a simmer over medium heat. Cook for 2–3 minutes, stirring often, until the sugar dissolves, then take off the heat. Place the orange slices in the hot sugar syrup, return to low heat and simmer gently for 30–45 minutes, until the pith is translucent. Remove from the heat and leave the orange slices to cool in the syrup.

4   Preheat the oven to 120°C. Line a baking tray with baking paper. Carefully transfer the orange slices to the lined tray and bake for 2 hours. Remove from the oven and cool on the tray. Cut each orange slice into wedges.

5   Place the whole orange in a heavy-based saucepan and cover with water. Bring to the boil over high heat, then reduce the heat to low and simmer for 2 hours, checking the water level from time to time and topping it up if needed. Take off the heat and cool the orange in the liquid. Preheat the oven to 150°C. Grease a square 20 cm cake tin with melted butter and line with baking paper.

6   Remove the orange and cut into quarters, discarding any seeds. Place the orange in a food processor and blend until smooth, then add the eggs and continue to blend until aerated and pale. Transfer to a bowl and mix in the ground almonds, sugar and baking powder. Spoon the mixture into the prepared tin and bake for 20 minutes, then rotate the tin and cook for a further 30 minutes. Remove from the oven and cool in the tin, then turn onto a large flat plate and cut into portions.

7   Serve with the ice-cream, raspberries and candied orange, dusted with icing sugar.

School Kitchen Gardens

It makes me so happy to see kitchen gardens popping up in schools right around Australia.

These gardens have so many benefits: kids get a firsthand look at the way fruit and vegetables grow and can then be cooked to make a meal; they work together to care for the plants, which teaches them the importance of teamwork; and they learn how to create something of value (using their new gardening and cooking knowledge), which builds basic business skills. And that's the real beauty of these gorgeous, functional gardens – they're so engaging that children hardly realise they're learning.

The Stephanie Alexander Kitchen Garden Program has led the way in teaching kids about food in a hands-on environment. It's a wonderful concept: they all get involved planting the seeds or seedlings, then they watch them grow and do all the tending that's required, from watering to weeding. Finally, the produce is ready to harvest, and the kids can see, smell, taste and then cook the food that has sprouted right before their eyes. Involving kids in this process broadens their outlook on food; they can see that it's not just something you buy in packets from the supermarket. They may even be more willing to try new things, and long-held stigmas about food (that brussels sprouts taste horrible, for example) can disappear.

John Velluti, of Velluti's, supplies me with the cream of the crop every time, and showed me around some school kitchen gardens he's involved with.

SCHOOL KITCHEN GARDENS

^ Preserved lemons

500 g cumquats

ice cubes

1 litre sugar syrup (see page 211)

Candied cumquats

Here is something you may not know – although cumquats are very sour, when you eat a whole one and chew the skin it becomes very sweet, very quickly. Amazing, isn't it! Of course, another way to sweeten them up is by candying.

Makes about 500 g

1 Bring a large saucepan of water to the boil over high heat. Add the cumquats and blanch for 30 seconds, then use a slotted spoon to remove and refresh in iced water. Repeat this process two more times.

2 Place the cumquats and sugar syrup in a heavy-based saucepan over low heat and simmer for 45 minutes to 1 hour, until the cumquats are tender and their skin is translucent. (Cooking the cumquats gently over low heat should prevent them bursting open.) Gently transfer to a sterilised jar and cover with the sugar syrup. Cool to room temperature, then seal the jar and store in a cool, dry place. Once opened, keep in the fridge.

500 g finger limes

ice cubes

1.5 litres sugar syrup (see page 211)

Candied finger limes

I reckon finger limes are the caviar of citrus – their flesh looks like tiny pearls, with the colour varying from bright-green to red, and they burst in your mouth. I love adding them to cocktails and other drinks.

Makes about 500 g

1 Bring a large saucepan of water to the boil over high heat. Add the finger limes and blanch for 1 minute, then use a slotted spoon to remove and refresh in iced water. Repeat this process two more times.

2 Place the finger limes and sugar syrup in a heavy-based saucepan over low heat and simmer for 45 minutes to 1 hour, until the finger limes are tender and their skin is translucent. Gently transfer to a sterilised jar and cover with the sugar syrup. Cool to room temperature, then seal the jar and store in a cool, dry place. Once opened, keep in the fridge.

1 kg pickling onions, peeled, leaving tips and roots intact so they retain their shape

1 litre pickling liquid (see page 208)

Pickled onions

Pickled onions are a fantastic ingredient to have on hand to serve with a platter or add to a salad. When you can get small pickling onions, buy them in bulk.

Makes about 1 kg

1 Cook the onions in a large saucepan of boiling water for 3–4 minutes or until beginning to soften, then drain and transfer to a sterilised jar. Bring the pickling liquid to a simmer, then pour over the onions to cover. Set aside for 10 minutes, then seal and store in a cool, dry place for at least 2 weeks before using (they will keep for several months). Once opened, keep in the fridge for up to 4 weeks.

500 g long red chillies, washed

1 litre pickling liquid (see page 208)

Pickled red chillies

This is a great way to preserve excess chillies from the garden.

Makes about 500 g

1 Place the chillies in a sterilised jar. Bring the pickling liquid to a simmer, then pour over the chillies to cover. Set aside for 10 minutes, then seal and store in a cool, dry place for at least 2–3 days before using (they will keep for up to 3 months). Once opened, keep in the fridge for up to 4 weeks.

^ Clockwise from top left: Pickled jalapeños,
Pickled green tomatoes, Pickled red chillies and Pickled onions

8 green tomatoes, washed and halved

100 g salt

1 litre pickling liquid (see page 208)

Pickled green tomatoes

These are a really lovely addition to sandwiches and salads.

Makes 16 pieces

1 Put the tomatoes on a tray. Toss with the salt and set aside for 15 minutes. Transfer to a bowl of cold water to wash off the excess salt, then drain and place in a sterilised jar.

2 Bring the pickling liquid to a simmer, then pour over the tomatoes to cover. Set aside for 10 minutes, then seal and store in a cool, dry place for at least 4 weeks before using (they will keep for several months). Once opened, keep in the fridge for up to 4 weeks.

500 g fresh jalapeño chillies, washed

1 litre pickling liquid (see page 208)

Pickled jalapeños

I have started growing jalapeños at home and love pickling them to serve in salads or with raw fish.

Makes about 500 g

1 Place the jalapeños in a sterilised jar. Bring the pickling liquid to a simmer, then pour over the jalapeños to cover. Set aside for 10 minutes, then seal and store in a cool, dry place for at least 2–3 days before using (they will keep for up to 3 months). Once opened, keep in the fridge for up to 4 weeks.

8

Basics

These simple preparations will make all
the difference to your cooking. I like to make
large quantities and freeze some, so that
I always have a flavour boost on hand
to enhance any meal.

2.5 kg chicken bones or wings

1 onion, roughly chopped

2 leeks, white part only, washed and roughly chopped

3 stalks celery, trimmed and roughly chopped

1 bulb garlic, cut in half crossways

1 bunch thyme

2 bay leaves

10 white peppercorns

Chicken stock

Whenever you make stock, I'd suggest making a big batch so you can freeze some. Then, when you're feeling poorly and in need of chicken soup (see page 95), it will be quicker and easier to make.

Makes 2 litres

1 Place the chicken bones or wings in a large heavy-based saucepan or stockpot and cover with water. Bring to the boil over high heat, then reduce the heat to low and skim off any scum that has risen to the surface.

2 Add the onion, leek, celery, garlic, thyme, bay leaves and peppercorns and gently simmer for 4 hours, skimming occasionally.

3 Strain through a fine-meshed sieve over a large heatproof bowl and set aside to cool. Store in the fridge for up to 4 days or in the freezer for several weeks.

1.6 litres chicken stock (see page 206)

1⅓ cups (330 ml) light soy sauce

200 ml rice wine vinegar

200 g caster sugar

10 g ginger, peeled and roughly chopped

2 star anise

3 cinnamon sticks

¼ cup (60 ml) sherry vinegar

2 small red chillies

wide strips of zest from 1 orange

1 bunch coriander, roots only

Master stock

I always have a master stock in my freezer. You can keep re-using it as this really intensifies the flavour. Just make sure you bring it to the boil each time. If it starts to evaporate, add more chicken stock.

Makes 2 litres

1 Place all the ingredients in a large heavy-based saucepan or stockpot and bring to a simmer over medium heat. Simmer for 20 minutes, then take off the heat and set aside for the flavours to infuse for 20 minutes. Strain through a fine-meshed sieve over a large heatproof bowl and set aside to cool. Store in the fridge for up to 4 days or in the freezer.

3 kg veal bones

1 tablespoon vegetable oil

1 onion, chopped

1 leek, white part only, washed and roughly chopped

1 stalk celery, chopped

1 carrot, chopped

½ bulb garlic, cut in half crossways

2 bay leaves

½ bunch thyme

1 teaspoon white peppercorns

300 ml red wine

Veal stock

This is a delicious basic stock that is really useful to have in your fridge or freezer.

Makes 3–4 litres

1 Preheat the oven to 160°C.

2 Place the veal bones on 2 large baking trays and roast for about 50 minutes or until golden brown.

3 Heat the vegetable oil in a large heavy-based saucepan or stockpot over medium heat. Add the onion, leek, celery, carrot, garlic, herbs and peppercorns and cook for 10–15 minutes or until the vegetables have softened and the onion is golden.

4 Deglaze the pan with the red wine, scraping all the sediment from the base of the pan, then add the roasted veal bones and cover with 5 litres cold water. Bring to a simmer, then reduce the heat to low and simmer gently for 4–5 hours, regularly skimming off any scum that rises to the surface. Strain through a fine-meshed sieve over a large heatproof bowl and set aside to cool. Store in the fridge up to 4 days or in the freezer for several weeks.

2 cups (500 ml) rice wine vinegar

1 cup (250 ml) chardonnay vinegar

150 g sugar

3 cm knob ginger, roughly chopped

2 tablespoons black peppercorns

1 tablespoon yellow mustard seeds

1 tablespoon salt

1 red chilli, halved lengthways

1 clove garlic

1 clove

Pickling liquid

Pickling liquid doesn't have to be complicated – it's just about mixing acid and sugar, then flavouring it with whatever you like.

Makes 2 litres

1   Place all the ingredients in a large heavy-based saucepan or stockpot with 1.2 litres water. Heat over medium–high heat for 10 minutes or until the liquid comes to the boil, then remove from the heat and strain through a fine-meshed sieve. Store in the fridge.

600 g table salt

400 g caster sugar

1 teaspoon black peppercorns

8 juniper berries

6 cloves

Brine

You can really taste the difference when meat or poultry is brined before it is cooked – there's more flavour and it is more succulent.

Makes 5 litres

1   Place all the ingredients in a heavy-based saucepan with 4 litres water and bring to the boil over high heat. Remove from the heat, strain through a fine-meshed sieve and store in the fridge. Do not use until cooled completely.

24 large roma tomatoes

ice cubes

100 ml extra virgin olive oil

1 leek, white part only, washed
and finely diced

2 cloves garlic, finely chopped

salt and pepper

Tomato sauce

This tomato sauce can be used for pasta sauces, pizza bases, to spoon over cooked meat or poultry, or just to serve as a condiment.

Makes 600 g

1 Score a cross in the base of each tomato. Bring a large saucepan of water to the boil. Add the tomatoes and leave for 20 seconds, then remove and place in a bowl of iced water. Peel away the skin of the tomatoes, then cut each tomato into quarters and remove the seeds. Finely dice the tomato flesh.

2 Heat the olive oil in a heavy-based saucepan over medium heat. Add the leek and garlic and saute for 2–3 minutes, until softened. Add the diced tomato and season with salt and pepper, to taste. Simmer for 10–15 minutes, until the sauce thickens. Take off the heat and set aside to cool. Store in the fridge for up to 5 days or in the freezer for several months.

---

2 cardamom pods

½ teaspoon cumin seeds

½ teaspoon coriander seeds

½ teaspoon fennel seeds

2½ tablespoons olive oil

½ onion, finely diced

2 cloves garlic, finely chopped

1 teaspoon tomato paste (puree)

2½ tablespoons white wine

400 g tomato sauce (see recipe above)

1 teaspoon sugar

Spiced tomato sauce

The addition of cardamom, cumin, coriander and fennel give just the right touch of spice to the basic tomato sauce recipe, above.

Makes 500 g

1 Remove the cardamom seeds from the pods; discard the pods. Toast the seeds in a dry non-stick frying pan until aromatic. Put all the spices into a mortar and pound with the pestle to a powder.

2 Heat the olive oil in a saucepan over medium–high heat. Add the onion and garlic and cook until the onion is softened, then add the ground spices and cook for 1 minute. Add the tomato paste and cook for 2 minutes, then pour in the wine and cook until it reduces to a glaze. Add the tomato sauce and cook over low heat for 20 minutes, until thickened. Add the sugar and season with salt and pepper, to taste. Take off the heat and set aside to cool. Store in the fridge for up to 5 days or in the freezer for several months.

100 ml vegetable oil

1 tablespoon sesame oil

1 golden shallot, thinly sliced

5 g ginger, peeled and cut into matchsticks

1 clove garlic, cut into matchsticks

25 g caster sugar

2 teaspoons soy sauce

1 teaspoon oyster sauce

1 teaspoon rice vinegar

Ginger and shallot sauce

Also known simply as '222', this was created many years ago for a staff lunch and has evolved into this beautiful aromatic sauce. It takes a little time to make, but it's worth the effort. It works well with just about everything, especially vegetables.

Makes about 150 ml

1   Place the oils, shallot and ginger in a small heavy-based saucepan over medium heat and cook for 10 minutes, until the shallot starts to caramelise. Add the garlic and cook for a further 2 minutes, until caramelised, then add the sugar and soy and oyster sauces and cook for 5 minutes more. Take off the heat and set aside to cool, then skim off roughly half the oil and discard. Mix in the vinegar and 1 teaspoon water and set aside to cool, then use a stick mixer to blend until smooth. Store in the fridge for up to 1 week.

25 ml chardonnay vinegar

25 ml champagne vinegar

3 teaspoons fresh lemon juice

1 teaspoon Dijon mustard

175 ml grapeseed oil

salt

Classic dressing

This is my standard salad dressing. It's simple and delicious.

Makes 1 cup (250 ml)

1   Whisk the vinegars, lemon juice and mustard in a small bowl until well combined. Slowly add the oil, whisking constantly, until it has all been added and the dressing is emulsified. Season with salt, to taste. Store in the fridge.

1 egg yolk

1 tablespoon white wine vinegar

1 teaspoon Dijon mustard

100 ml grapeseed oil

salt and pepper

Mayonnaise

Home-made mayo is incomparable. If it splits, just grab another egg yolk and slowly whisk it in – this will bring it back together.

Makes 200 g

1 Whisk the egg yolk, vinegar and mustard in a small mixing bowl until combined. Slowly add the oil, whisking constantly, until it has all been added and the dressing is emulsified. Season with salt and pepper, to taste. Store in the fridge for up to 4 days.

500 g caster sugar

Sugar syrup

Make sugar syrup as you need it, because it doesn't freeze well due to the high sugar content. You can make less if you like, just keep the ratio of sugar to water at 1:2.

Makes 1 litre

1 Place the sugar in a heavy-based saucepan with 1 litre water and bring to the boil over medium heat, stirring until the sugar dissolves. Remove from the heat and set aside to cool. Store in the fridge.

Acknowledgements

A big thank you to the amazing MorSul staff, in particular all my head chefs: Ben Turner, Ben Russell, Richie Dolan, Leena D'Onofrio, Richard Slarp and Andrew Honeysett.

Thanks also to my trusted suppliers: Anthony, Anita and Vic Puharich from Vic's Premium Quality Meat; John and Bree Velluti from Velluti's – The Fruit and Veg Company; Kevin and Louie from M&G Seafood; and Jules Crocker from Joto Fresh Fish.

At Penguin, I'd like to thank Julie Gibbs, publishing director, for her great support over four years and four cookbooks; Anna Scobie, editor; Emily O'Neill, designer; Katrina O'Brien, publishing manager; and Charlotte Bachali, publishing assistant.

Thanks to photographer Rob Palmer, photo-shoot producer Cass Stokes and stylist Vanessa Austin for capturing the food so beautifully.

I'd also like to thank Peter Sullivan, Bruce Solomon, Susan Sullivan and of course my family, Sarah, Harry, Amelia, Freddy and Sanchez, for their understanding and support. And a special thanks to Simon Sandall and Laura Baratto – without the help of these two this book wouldn't exist.

Index

LANTERN

Published by the Penguin Group
Penguin Group (Australia)
707 Collins Street, Melbourne, Victoria 3008, Australia
(a division of Penguin Australia Pty Ltd)
Penguin Group (USA) Inc.
375 Hudson Street, New York, New York 10014, USA
Penguin Group (Canada)
90 Eglinton Avenue East, Suite 700, Toronto, Canada ON M4P 2Y3
(a division of Pearson Penguin Canada Inc.)
Penguin Books Ltd
80 Strand, London WC2R 0RL England
Penguin Ireland
25 St Stephen's Green, Dublin 2, Ireland
(a division of Penguin Books Ltd)
Penguin Books India Pvt Ltd
11 Community Centre, Panchsheel Park, New Delhi – 110 017, India
Penguin Group (NZ)
67 Apollo Drive, Rosedale, Auckland 0632, New Zealand
(a division of Pearson New Zealand Ltd)
Penguin Books (South Africa) (Pty) Ltd, Rosebank Office Park, Block D,
181 Jan Smuts Avenue, Parktown North, Johannesburg, 2196, South Africa
Penguin (Beijing) Ltd
7F, Tower B, Jiaming Center, 27 East Third Ring Road North,
Chaoyang District, Beijing 100020, China

Penguin Books Ltd, Registered Offices: 80 Strand, London, WC2R 0RL, England

First published by Penguin Group (Australia), 2014

1 3 5 7 9 10 8 6 4 2

Text copyright © Matt Moran 2014
Photography copyright © Rob Palmer 2014

The moral right of the author has been asserted.

Design by Emily O'Neill © Penguin Group (Australia)
Photography by Rob Palmer
Styling for food photography by Vanessa Austin
Typeset by Post Pre-press Group, Brisbane, Queensland
Colour separation by Splitting Image Colour Studio, Clayton, Victoria
Printed and bound in China by 1010 Printing International Limited

National Library of Australia
Cataloguing-in-Publication data:

Moran, Matt, author.
Matt's kitchen garden cookbook / Matt Moran; Rob Palmer, photographer.
ISBN: 9781921383618 (hardback).
Includes index.
Cooking. Food–Australia. Kitchen gardens–Australia.
Other Authors/Contributors: Palmer, Rob, photographer.

641.5994

penguin.com.au/lantern